God with Us

Stories of Christmas

God with Us

Stories of Christmas

by
David Ruhe

David Ruhe

Plymouth Congregational
United Church of Christ
Des Moines, Iowa

Edited by Kendra L. Williams.

Cover design by Cindy Eaton-Eklund.

Book design by Mary Y. Nilsen, Zion Publishing, www.zionpublishing.org.

ISBN-13: 978-1502595249
ISBN-10: 1502595249

Plymouth Congregational United Church of Christ
4126 Ingersoll Avenue
Des Moines, Iowa 50312
515-255-3149

Printed in the United States of America

Table of Contents

Introduction— 7

1994 "And the Word Became Flesh"— 15

1995 "The Light"— 28

1996 "Here and Now"— 41

1997 "The Surprise"— 53

1998 "*In Transit Gloria*"— 65

1999 "Hopes and Fears"— 76

2000 "Angel's Song"— 87

2001 "The Plan B Carol"— 99

2002 "The Guest Room"— 110

2003 "The More Things Change"— 121

2004 "Out Back"— 134

2005 "You Never Know"— 147

2006 "Candlelight Story"— 158

2007 "The Pageant"— 168

2008 "Holy Night"— 180

2009 "All the Best"— 190

2010 "Born a Savior"— 201

2011 "The Gift"— 213

2012 "Every Heart"— 221

2013 "All Things New"— 233

Introduction

I love Christmas. It seems silly to say that so baldly, but it really is where all of this begins for me. I love the decorations, the music—even the anticipatory frenzy connects with me on some level. I confess to being entertained by the brazen commercialism surrounding Christmas, ranging as it does from the ridiculous to the obscene. Somehow, it seems like our lives on steroids.

But I hope I love it mostly because of what God does in and through it all, both apart from and in the very midst of our versions of Christmas. In the most profoundly mysterious way, God becomes present in our lives. Often against the backdrop of life gone awry, we become aware that God is with us, and somehow everything is transformed. That simple assertion is what every one of these stories is about.

"God is with us." As a prosaic pronouncement, that doesn't sound like very much. But as a startling and wonderful surprise that catches us in the middle of life's dramas—great or small—it can mean everything. It means we are not alone. It means that our lives have meaning and purpose. It means that the sometimes desperately difficult calling to love one another is perhaps not impossible, after all. It means that our deepest yearnings are fulfilled in the here-and-now of everyday life, if we can figure out how to pay attention. It means, as the shepherds of Luke 2 heard it so long ago, "Do not be afraid."

See what I mean? So many words. Blah, blah, blah. That's why Christmas is a time for stories, for telling as truthfully and simply as we can how God comes to be present in the midst of life—any life, every life, your life and mine. That's all these stories try to do.

I'm not completely convinced it's a good idea to publish them in this form. They were written to be heard by candlelight on Christmas Eve. I've always felt that their context within a worship service allowed these stories to be understated in a way that might not translate to the written page. By design, many of them don't even try to end with a "Wow!" but with a "Huh?" The music in the services has always been so absolutely crucial an element that the stories may feel hopelessly incomplete without it.

Even the three-section format in which each of these stories is written is designed to work in a specific context: worship among people who are likely to have short attention spans and to be a bit ill at ease in church. I don't mean that to sound unkind at all. They are there. Somehow they know Christmas is important. If for whatever reason you feel you have to pick just two, Easter and Christmas are the right ones, to be sure.

And Christmas Eve has its own magic that has always been a part of the context of these stories, a strange Christmas concoction of memory and anticipation. Whatever our family situation, it is accentuated on Christmas Eve: families are united, joyfully or tentatively; or they are divided by conflict, circumstance or death. Christmas Eve is a time when we take stock of things—we can't help it, which is why some people absolutely hate Christmas and go to great lengths to flee into distractions. Everything is more intense at Christmas. We may think of it as life with the volume turned up, but maybe it's really life with the volume turned way down. The silence is unexpected and almost terrifying. But, "do not be afraid."

And so I wonder how, if at all, this translates onto the page. But then, I've almost never been confident that these stories would connect with anybody, period. I have learned simply to bring them as an offering and to hope that they enhance, deepen or even disrupt in a good way somebody else's experience of Christmas. I am almost always surprised when somebody tells me that a story has touched them. I find this deeply mysterious. But they invariably touch me very deeply when I write them, and I often cry when I reread them.

People often ask me where these stories come from, and I usually tell them I don't know—which is not a deliberate attempt to be dishonest. But I do know that they come from the raw material of my life, my experience. We write what we know. Sometimes they recount events as directly as I can recall them, with names changed to protect the innocent. But mostly they are more purely fictional, telling the stories of real people who are not actual persons; rather they are composites of people I have known, made-up from memorable personalities or types who are plunked down into a situation that seems real or at least plausible to me.

And then they take on a life of their own. I don't know how this happens, really, but they emerge from memory to take on a new form that surprises me, becoming sassy or disappointing or heartbreakingly tender in ways I would not have expected. I almost always visualize very clearly the places in my stories, and I think I know pretty precisely the life situation as I begin to write. But what exactly the people will do or say is something I discover. None of us really knows what we will do when God shows up.

Ideas for these stories come from anywhere and everywhere and at any time. For awhile, I had a Christmas Story Ideas file into which I would jam scribbled notes from time to time. Most of these proved utterly unintelligible (if not illegible) when I returned to them later, whatever magic I had thought I sensed having long passed its expiration date. But at times I have had a surplus of ideas. I don't remember ever abandoning a story once I started it, but some of them have been a real wrestling match. Most often they arrive in a flurry and are written down rather quickly with more extensive editing coming only later. I experience this sudden arrival of a story as a visitation, and I have learned to wait for it. Once I wrote one in the car when I was bringing our son Paul home from college for Christmas vacation. (He was driving.)

I feel a bit apologetic about the fact that these stories draw from the same limited data base—my life. I have not really attempted to climb into the experience of someone terribly different from me, not from sloth so much as from the justifiable suspicion that I would do this very badly. So if there is an alienating sameness of race, social class, sexual orientation, education and family circumstance that runs through all these stories, please consider the limitations of the source. I wish these stories were more universally hospitable than they are. Given their intent, they ought to be.

All these stories are about the same thing, really. Families or individuals of many shapes, sizes and configurations are confronted with problems, real or imagined, which they approach with their unique combinations of belief and unbelief. Sometimes they tell lies—to themselves and to one another—but they inevitably end up discovering a truth. That truth is that God comes into the midst of life to say "I love you" to each of us and all of us, and to say it in a way we cannot ignore, catching us at our most vulnerable by speaking through the helplessness of taking on human form. This does not magically transform our circumstances, but it does transform us. It's the same story, over and over, but it comes to each of us in a new way many times throughout our lives. My stories may seem (and be!) hackneyed and formulaic, but the story is always new.

In the brief introduction to the individual stories, I will share what I reasonably can of the life experience underlying that particular story. I do this with a bit of trepidation—not just because I am afraid that some readers will see themselves (wrongly) as the precise subject of the story, but because by pulling back the curtain just a bit on where these stories come from, I hope to encourage you to see your own life as a story through which God is constantly being revealed. Sometimes fiction is the best vehicle for approaching the deepest truths. In that sense, your life is the stuff of fiction, too.

Many thanks to the good people of Plymouth Congregational United Church of Christ in Des Moines, Iowa, where these stories were written and shared. We have had 20 Christmases together. For me, they have been 20 moving reminders that God is with us.

David Ruhe
June 2013

1994

This first Des Moines story was actually born of an experience I had while I was working in Omaha. A family in the church there had some relatives who were killed in a head-on collision in Kansas City, leaving three young boys orphaned. I was asked to go Kansas City to assist with the funeral and to help the family sort out what would become of the children. When the funeral was over, I left for Omaha and got caught in a terrible snowstorm, just as described here. I made it to St. Joseph, Missouri, where I did in fact get the last room at the Holiday Inn—though it was not the bridal suite (description of which is based on the Villa Madrid Motel in Crete, Nebraska), and I did not ultimately end up sharing it with strangers. Utterly unprepared to spend that night in St. Joseph, I did end up "paying myself a visit."

"And the Word Became Flesh"

Part I

As snow and ice beat on the windshield of her tiny Toyota, Sarah struggled to avoid being mesmerized by the hypnotic slap of the wipers. Periodically the wintry onslaught would become overwhelming, and she would have to roll down the window and reach out awkwardly with a long-handled scraper to free the besieged blades. Sarah couldn't manage more than 15 miles per hour...but she didn't dare stop on the interstate. It was crazy. It was scary. What had been rain in Kansas City had become more and more menacing as she drove north. A section of the drive that under better conditions would require an hour had already taken more than three. It was terribly hard just to see the road. And it was getting worse by the minute.

But the hauntingly helpless plight of vehicles stalled and stranded along the way made Sarah all the more determined not to join their number. Her only hope was to keep going.

Sarah didn't need this. Not today. Only a week before Christmas, this trip to Kansas City for the funeral of a college friend was supposed to be a one-day excursion. She had brought no boots, no toothbrush, no plans to be stuck anywhere. Her grip on the steering wheel, knuckles white from the tension, betrayed her growing anxiety as the storm deepened.

It is beautiful, she thought. The surreal quiet and the blinding blizzard created almost an atmosphere of sensory deprivation, and her mind raced to fill the void:

So much to do… I've got to get home this evening… Steve will be home from school in two days—Two DAYS!!—and I know how much he's counting on having Christmas the way it's always been. I don't even have a tree yet. This divorce has been hard for him, especially being away. This first year without both parents at home is going to be tough…He's always been a real nut about Christmas. I remember that day when he was 6, and I found him carefully counting out his underwear in a tidy pile on the bed. He said he was trying to figure out which would be his Christmas underwear this year! And then the time he... What's that red light? It's another truck—that one's stuck on the median, don't follow him! I can't even see the road here…there's an overpass...better just aim between the pillars there. Where in the world am I? It seems like hours since the last sign… Oh, there's one: What does that say? Lamoni?! Am I only to Lamoni? At this rate, I'll never get back in daylight, and…

A surge of adrenaline shot through her as the car began to swerve. From behind came the sound of a horn, and suddenly, out of nowhere, a large pickup with huge tires emerged from the featureless white and shot past her, kicking up a load of ice that immobilized the hapless wipers yet again. As she lowered the window and fought to clear the windshield one more time, a green exit sign gradually materialized in her view, almost like a command.

The friendly woman at the Visitors Center directed Sarah to a motel that had exactly one room left—maybe the last room in town. And was she ever glad to have it! "We don't usually rent this one out in the winter time? It's for special occasions? Costs extra?" the cheerfully opportunistic manager had announced. Even his annoying habit of making every statement sound like a question failed to dampen Sarah's sense of good fortune. "But what the heck? A storm like this is a special occasion?"

"This one" turned out to be the bridal suite: everything you might imagine, and more. There was inch-thick purple shag carpet on the floor, vintage 1978. The artificial fur bedspread on the king-sized water bed was evidently designed to enhance animal magnetism—though Sarah did not allow herself to imagine just what sort of animals it might have attracted in its day. A white Naugahyde sofa somehow failed to provide the homey touch for which it was intended. But this was home enough for now...in fact, it was sanctuary.

Most disconcerting, however, were the hanging, rheostat-controlled, pseudo-crystal chandelier and two walls of design-etched mirrored tiles that gave Sarah the constant sensation of being watched. When she situated herself at the desk, which faced directly into yet another mirror, she could see the reflection behind of a smaller self sitting at a smaller desk and peering into a smaller mirror which yielded an image of a still smaller self, desk and mirror...and so on to microscopic infinity. The funeral had been taste enough of eternity; Sarah managed to position herself so that she would not be "beset behind and before" by her own image.

The surprise problem was—nothing to do. After she had phoned the neighbors and asked them to let out the dog; after she had called work and told them not to expect her until later the next day; after the problem of food had been solved through a raiding of the cheese, sausage and crackers she had picked up at the Plaza for Friday's party; and with a little lift to the spirits provided from the bottle of scotch procured for the same purpose; Sarah had to pass the time. List-making on yellowed motel stationery didn't take very long, and it wasn't very satisfying to identify a zillion and one tasks that needed doing when she couldn't do anything about them. The TV managed to bring in two stations, one of which was Oprah and the other might as well have been. She was stuck.

So that is how it came to pass in those days that Sarah found herself adrift on an ocean of artificial fur, surrounded by reflections of her own image, and sipping scotch in the unaccustomed company of Gideon's Bible. "All right, Gideon," she said almost out loud. "Let's you and me have a little Christmas party of our own."

Part II

Gideon, as it turned out, was full of surprises. How many Christmas pageants had Sarah been through over the years? She had thought she had a pretty good handle on the Christmas story, so she plunged right into the first Gospel, Matthew. But after half a chapter of "begats," she came across a strangely unfamiliar story of Joseph trying to decide what to do about his pregnant fiancée. The footnote said he was agonizing over whether to have her stoned to death—the prescribed punishment for adultery. "Well," Sarah thought, "that would have been a different sort of ending! We skipped over that part in Sunday school!" As she read on, she came to the familiar story about the Wise Men, the Three Kings of Orient Are. But she began to look for where it says that there are three. It doesn't. Or, for that matter, where it says that they are kings.

And where it says that their names were Gaspar, Balthazar and Melchior. It doesn't. Worst of all, when the Wise Men arrive at Bethlehem (presumably where Mary and Joseph lived, because there is no story in Matthew of a Roman census or a journey from Nazareth) they go not to a stable and a manger, but to a house. A house! Wait a minute, here! And then this bizarre Herod person shows up and goes into a rage, killing children. Even though the Wise Men are warned in a dream not to return to Herod, and Joseph is warned in a dream to flee to Egypt—why didn't all the other kids' parents get dreams, too? This was supposed to be comforting and familiar.

Mark was next. But Mark doesn't even mention Jesus' birth, or say anything about where he came from. Suddenly he just appears, to be baptized by John the Baptist, and the breathless narrative of Mark moves off so quickly, there is no possibility of flagging it down to ask a question about Jesus' birth. By this time, Sarah began to suspect that she was onto something.

Next comes Luke, the opposite extreme. A long first chapter tells not only about the events leading up to Jesus' birth, but all about John the Baptist, too. Angels keep showing up and scaring the stuffing out of people: Zechariah, Mary, the shepherds—and then telling them not to be afraid. And everybody sings: Mary sings, Zechariah sings, the angels sing, Anna and Simeon sing about the wonderful things Jesus will do. It's more like an opera than a Gospel.

"This is the one I know," Sarah thought as she hit the familiar words of Luke's second chapter, "In those days a decree went out from Caesar Augustus that all the world should be taxed...." But even here there were surprises: shepherds, yes; but no wise men. No star, no drummer boy, no talking animals. "These Gospels," she actually said out loud to nobody, "are each different stories. These people had different ideas about how to describe Jesus coming into the world." And she found, as if for the first time, this mysterious and wonderful summary of Mary's response to the shepherds' news of singing angels: "But Mary kept all these things, and pondered them in her heart." There's more here of mystery than of majesty.

But the Gospel According to John was the biggest surprise of all: no story—not even a stab at history—just a theological treatise that at first was very difficult to read. But for some reason—maybe the scotch—this time it began to make some sense. "In the beginning was the Word," she began to read, not trying to figure the words out one by one, but letting them wash over her, letting key images and phrases shine forth like shooting stars: "In him was light...The light shines in the darkness, and the darkness did not overcome it...He came to his own, and his own people did not accept him... And the Word became flesh, and dwelt among us...."

Quietly, and very slowly at first, Sarah began to cry, the tears trickling gently down her face, falling onto her hands as she held the book before her. "That's what this is about. It isn't about all the neat and tidy and magazine-perfect things we talk about at Christmas. Family? This is a story of pregnancy out of wedlock. Hearth and home? These are homeless refugees. Peace and tranquility? There's a homicidal maniac in here. Tradition? This is outside the lines, God doing something totally new. We look to Christmas for peaceful reassurance. Mary and Joseph are yanked around by Rome and by Herod. Grandeur and glory? This is simplicity and mystery. I don't have to make things perfect to have Christmas. Christmas is God coming into this world, just as it is: not all tidied up and shiny...a world where divorce happens and people who shouldn't die, die. "And the Word became flesh and lived among us...." not because we made it perfect first, but because that's what God is like.

Sarah's gentle, silent tears had become sobs by the time

the phone rang. The sound was so unexpected that she almost couldn't place it at first. It was the front desk.

"'Scuse me, ma'am? Sorry to bother you? But I just got a call from Verniece over at the welcome center? They's been tryin' to help out with the stranded folks over there, and a bunch of 'em's been put up in people's homes in town? But she was wonderin'... there's a lady here with a little kid? And when she asked if we had any space at all, I thought about you all by your lonesome in that big room and thought they should stay with you." His sudden abandonment of question mode made this seem less a request than a command. But it didn't matter. Sarah was fresh from reading about inns with no room...there would be room in this one. Quickly, she wiped her nose on her sleeve and tried to sound composed. "Certainly. You just send those poor folks right on up."

Part III

The sun was shining brightly, and the crisp and clear morning was a winter wonderland as Sarah turned off the interstate and drove the two miles to home. But with the familiar streets came familiar thoughts. She felt, like a sudden chill, the awareness of demands—work and the holidays—and with it the all too familiar tension that seemed her constant companion. She resolved instead to think back over the events of the preceding day. Hard to believe it was just about this time yesterday when the funeral ended and she began her trip home.

Of all of it—the storm, the bridal suite, the close encounter with Gideon—certainly the most wonderful were the woman and child who had ended up being her companions for the night. She had welcomed them thinking that she was doing something for them. They did much more for her. They were fleeing an abusive husband and father. Slowed by the storm, they had run out of gas and money just as they got to the same exit that had been Sarah's refuge. But the woman's determination was the most amazing part. She had been through so much, but she was so calm about it. She made Sarah's troubles seem somehow more manageable. Sarah resolved not to forget what she had learned: that life, with all its imperfections, is a gift to be received, more than a project to be perfected.

As she turned onto her street and headed home for a change of clothes, Sarah could see even from the corner that her driveway had been shoveled. "Well," she thought, "that solves the problem of no boots. But who did the shoveling?" As she turned into the driveway, there was her son, Steve, shovel in hand, just finishing up the front steps.

"Hi, Mom!" he said breathlessly, and without putting down the shovel gave her a one-armed hug. "I got a ride from one of the guys. We left early to beat the storm. I thought I'd make myself useful. Mrs. Zwiegert next door told me about your adventure coming home from Kansas City."

"Mrs. Zwiegert doesn't know the half of it," Sarah responded. "Have I got a story to tell you. But that can wait. Are you hungry?"

"Are you kidding? I'm always hungry!"

Over lunch, the first rush of news from the semester's ending gradually gave way to an uneasy silence. As Steve finished his sandwich he said, "Mom, I've noticed that there isn't a tree up yet, and…"

"Steve," Sarah interrupted defensively, "I'm sorry. I haven't had the chance to get it done. I've been really busy, but I don't seem to be as productive as I used to be. It's taken a lot of energy just adjusting to living alone. But I think I've got it all figured out how we can do all the Christmas things you love."

"Mom," Steve replied, "I've been thinking a lot about this Christmas. And I know it's going to be different. It has to be. And that's OK. I'll go over to Dad's apartment on Christmas Eve, and then we'll have the day together on Christmas. But we don't have to try to do everything as though nothing had happened. At least it'll be real. Sometimes I got the feeling that we were using Christmas to try to make everything else all right. If I can have the car this afternoon, I'll get us a tree. But let's not worry about trying to do all the stuff this year. We don't have to have a perfect Christmas; let's just have this one."

1995

During the early 1970s, the Arab oil embargo precipitated an energy crisis, resulting in long lines at gas stations and a host of efforts—most of them short-lived—to conserve energy. For a time, churches that illuminated their steeples at night were asked to turn their lights out in support of conservation efforts. I remember vividly reading an editorial by The Rev. Nathanael Guptill, Connecticut Conference Minister of the United Church of Christ, encouraging the churches to support most conservation efforts, but to let their lights shine for at least a while each evening as a sign of hope. This story shares something of that spirit. The church described is the Berlin Congregational Church, where I served when I was a student at Yale Divinity School. Every detail of that building is vivid in my memory even today. The church people are influenced by a mix of characters from Berlin, Branford and

Omaha, but mostly they are the products of my imagination. The part about preparing casseroles for the student minister whose mother died describes what the Berlin Church did for me in April 1973.

"The Light"

Part I

Well, I suppose that blasted mall finally was good for something, Harold Lowell conceded to himself as he turned out of the parking lot to make the familiar drive to the church. His reliable bright yellow 1972 Lincoln Town Car monopolized the street, rolling along with elaborate majesty like the Queen Mary. The contrast was still a jolt as one drove from the new and brightly lit mall at the edge of town and crossed into the Brighton Historical District, where street lights were small, dim and widely spaced, and houses looked pretty much as they had for generations. At the center of the Historical District stood the church, which still looked pretty good, considering the neglect it had received in recent years.

At the mall, lights glared and music blared in the final frenzied crush of procrastinators. But in the older, stately sections of town, people were more discrete in their observance of Christmas Eve. In many of the houses, there was a single electric candle in each of the front windows, lending a gentle sense of serenity and welcome. People in the Brighton Historical District didn't go in for casino-style flashing lights or elaborate lawn decorations.

For many years, the most prominent feature of the Brighton skyline—if you could call it that—was the church. To the first-time visitor, the church building appeared to be all out of proportion, with the steeple much too large for the rest of it. The front doors to the sanctuary opened through the base of the steeple, which reached some seven stories into the air. The rest of the narrow, two-story building seemed inadequate to keep the whole thing from tipping over in a strong wind. Somewhere about three stories up, there was a clock which the locals claimed to be on God's time; it had long since stopped working. At the very pinnacle was a weather-vane, testimony to the first great congregational dispute, between those who thought a cross should be up there and those who thought otherwise. Otherwise won out; those who wanted a cross started their own church across town.

For much of its majestic life, the steeple of the Brighton Church was lighted at night and was visible for miles around. But with the influx of commercial development, the Brighton mall had become a more familiar landmark, and the sleepy little town, with the exception of the small historical district, joined the 20th century with a vengeance. They turned out the steeple lights during the energy crisis in 1973, when the Arab oil embargo stimulated long lines at the gas pumps and year-round daylight savings time, and when Harold Lowell got an excellent price on his gas-guzzling Lincoln Town Car.

And the steeple had remained dark. The church declined and struggled. First, they dropped their Christian Education director and made do with volunteers. Then, the part-time organist and choir director gave way to Mrs. Bradburn, who claimed to have once been a music teacher.

Next, the minister went to part time. And now they were down to 54 members, with a succession of students from the seminary who came in to do the preaching on Sundays and the occasional funeral. Nobody could remember the last wedding.

Sometimes, the divinity students were pretty good, and sometimes not. But the dwindling congregation had learned not to count on them too much, except to do the big things, like Christmas Eve.

Their present student minister, Steve Harris, was one of the good ones, which meant that he didn't try to change the words to all the Christmas carols. But two days earlier, he had called to say that his mother had died in Chicago, and he would be going home for the funeral on Christmas Eve. The president of the congregation was Jennifer Stearns, a know-nothing newcomer single mother who, at the annual meeting, had been the only one willing to take the position. When she got the call from Steve, for some unknown reason she took her election seriously and thought she had to do something. She had made a few phone calls and decided to cancel the Christmas Eve service. Nobody spoke up to object at the time, but she just should have known better.

So now it seemed to be up to Harold. They had had a service on Christmas Eve all the years he and Erma had been raising their children. This was the first year he was without her, and for a time he had managed to convince himself that Christmas Eve didn't matter. But suddenly, as he sat watching some stupid football game on television that afternoon, it had mattered a great deal. If this was the year there would be no service, at least somebody had to make a statement.

The car door closed with a reassuringly deep and familiar "thunk!" and Harold made his way through the snow on the front lawn of the church. He had to dig around a little bit, but he found them easily enough: The flood lights were still there, all right. Kids had long since removed the bulbs for ammunition for excursions into vandalism, but the fixtures were still basically sound. Harold had trimmed the grass around them enough times to know that. Fumbling with the huge plastic bag and removing the elaborate cardboard encasement for the bulbs, one by one he screwed them in and made some effort at aiming them. "Here goes nothing," he thought, as he made his way toward the building to find the switch.

He knew his way in the dark: key a quarter turn to the right, in the door, turn left, down four stairs, around to the right, through a doorway, through the church school room, into a small corridor on the left. There was a pull cord hanging down. Yep, there it was. As the light came on he turned to the left. There behind an accordion style folding door, next to the old fuse box, was the switch. He flipped it on.

Even from inside, he could tell that it worked. The dark basement windows were suddenly awash with light. "Well, how about that!" he chuckled to himself. "Now let's tune this thing up a little bit."

He was back out on the lawn, trying to aim the rusted fixtures in a way that would show off the steeple to best effect, when the first car drove up. It was Ed and Sue Groves on their way home from dinner at the Pancake House down on the old highway. "Harold," Ed called out. "What the Sam Hill are you doing out there in the snow? And who the heck turned those lights on?"

"What does it look like I'm doing? I'm aiming the lights.

You want to help, or just criticize?"

"Well, I..."

"You got any WD-40 in that tool box you always carry in your trunk? These puppies are pretty rusty."

It took them awhile. But between the two of them, and with Sue's artistic eye, they did a pretty passable job of getting some light on the old steeple. Then they went inside the church to wash up from the cold and messy work. That's when the phone rang. Harold picked it up.

"Yep...Well, it's Harold...Yep...I did it...I don't know, but it just seemed to me that it was Christmas Eve and somebody ought to do something, so I did...Nope, just did it on my own. Ed came by and helped me...I suppose I'll pay the electric bill if nobody else wants to."

Then he paused. "Well, sure," he said at last, with a twinkle in his eye, "let's make it 8 o'clock... That's right... well, you just get on the phone and spread the word. Call Ellie Farrell, she'll get the news around faster than anybody else. Just tell them the Christmas Eve service will be at 8 o'clock. OK."

Harold hung up the phone and turned to Ed. "Well, Ed, it looks as though you and I have some work to do."

Part II

At first, it went just fine. There wasn't time even to think about getting the drafty old sanctuary warm. So they set things up downstairs in the fellowship hall outside the kitchen. There was an old folding table, and Sue knew where the table cloths were kept. They found one of the poinsettias left over from Sunday morning. Nearby in a storeroom was a wooden cross—a relic from the days when there used to be a church school. And they found a wicker basket, in case they felt like taking an offering.

Pretty soon things were ready, the metal folding chairs arranged in two groups with a center aisle. In less than an hour and a half, word shot around the small community and much of the regular congregation began to gather. They were not very demonstrative folks. But it was evident that they were excited, like children who were getting away with something and embarking on a great adventure.

The first part was easy. They knew that they had to sing "Hark the Herald Angels Sing." The service always started with that. Since Mrs. Bradburn showed up to play the piano, everybody knew that they would have to sit through her playing and singing of "O Holy Night," so that happened. She hadn't had time to practice, but it wouldn't have made much difference. Harold knew where to find the Christmas story about the shepherds and the angels in Luke 2, so he read that. And he did a very nice job with prayer concerns, asking the gathered folks if there was anything in particular on their minds this evening. They prayed in silence for the people and things that were mentioned: illnesses and travel. As an afterthought, somebody mentioned Steve Harris and his mother's funeral. Then they said the Lord's Prayer. All of that took about 15 minutes.

And then they didn't know quite what to do. They had barely taken the chill off the metal chairs, and Harold was out of ideas. He was just about to suggest that they sing "Silent Night" and break into the Christmas cookies that several people had brought when he looked up and saw Jennifer Stearns standing in the doorway with her son, Matthew. Even though she was the president of the congregation, she just wasn't on anybody's mental list of folks who should be called about the service. She had seen the light on the steeple and come to investigate. Once she saw all the cars, she had a pretty good idea that something was happening.

They could tell right away that she was hurt. "What is going on here?" she asked. The room was silent, as though they had been caught with their collective hand in the cookie jar. She asked again, not scoldingly, but imploringly. "Will somebody please tell me what is happening here? Whose idea was this?"

Finally Harold spoke up. "I suppose it was sort of my idea. At least turning on the light was my idea, and then one thing sort of led to another and, well, here we are. This is where we're supposed to be. We've always had church on Christmas Eve, and we didn't think that a little thing like the student minister being gone ought to make any difference."

Jennifer looked exasperated. "I think it's wonderful that you want to be in church on Christmas Eve. But where were all of you when the decision had to be made? Why didn't somebody just speak up and say something? Why did you leave me out on the limb all by myself and then punish me for making what you obviously consider the wrong decision by not even inviting me when you decided to have a service? I suppose it's fine with you for somebody younger to come along to do all the work, to see that the bills get paid and keep things running. And I am happy enough to do it. But then why do you act like this? You don't want to be a church. You want to be a little club that keeps things the way they've always been in the past, an exclusive little group that holds off change and drives away new people. You think you're trying to keep things going, but really you're making sure that they're going to die. Do you think that stupid spotlight makes this a church?"

Jennifer hadn't even noticed that her son was tugging at her coat, trying to get her to shut up and let these people do their Christmas thing, trying to stop her tirade before she had alienated absolutely everybody in the whole town. But somewhere along the line he had stopped. It seemed too late.

Once again an awkward silence filled the room. Sue Groves finally spoke. "Jennifer," she said, "I don't really blame you for being upset. It wasn't very nice of us not to call you, at least. But we're not here to spite you. We're here because we need to be here or it isn't quite Christmas. And even though there aren't as many of us as there used to be, and even though we don't have a minister any more, and even though we're pretty much preoccupied with our own aches and pains, I guess, this place holds a lot of memories for us, and there is something here that is very much alive."

"I know there is," Jennifer responded at last. "I'm sorry I said all those things… I don't really mean them. I know that this really is a church. I guess I just wanted to be a part of it, too."

Part III

At some point, the conversation took a turn. Probably it was when somebody suggested that they break into the cookies. They stood around as they had countless times before, eating cookies and drinking coffee—the sort of informal communion that is the real lifeblood of a lot of congregations. Except that instead of breaking into little clusters of close friends the way they always did, this time they remained a group of the whole. At first, they talked about the way things used to be, sharing Christmas memories, telling about how they used to have a big Christmas tree in the sanctuary, and how for years and years Conrad Baldwin had to be the one to light the star on Christmas Eve. They remembered how the children used to put on a pageant at Christmas and the year the choir did that wonderful Fred Waring arrangement with narration that had everybody in tears at the end.

It went on like that for a while, before somebody—maybe it was Sue Groves, maybe not—wondered out loud if there wasn't something they could do for Steve Harris, and somebody else came up with the idea of casseroles. Almost before you knew it, they had about a dozen people signed up to prepare things that could be put in his freezer and that would be waiting for him when he got back. A sympathy card was produced from somebody's very large all-purpose purse and passed around and signed.

They didn't exactly resolve anything, but they sure felt a lot more comfortable together. Jennifer apologized again for her outburst, and everybody said that of course they would have felt the same way, and maybe they should think about how they treat new people. But not much came of that conversation. After awhile, things seemed to sort of resolve themselves, and Jennifer had this idea come to her that maybe they should sing "Silent Night" after all, as a kind of benediction. But she didn't say anything, and she was glad she didn't, because pretty soon Ed Groves spoke up and said, "Well, got to go now. We've got to get up in the morning and drive to our daughter's. Merry Christmas, everybody!" And they all said, "Merry Christmas!" and drifted away.

It happened that Jennifer was among the last to leave, having remained to help clean up. As they were about to go out the door, they met Harold on his way back in. "Well," he said, "I guess this sort of worked out OK. I came back to do something about the light. Do you want me to turn it off?" He pointed to the outside.

Jennifer knew enough not to blow this one. "Oh," she said, "let's just leave it on for now." So they did.

1996

The saints of God come in all shapes and sizes. The character of Cat here is based not-so-loosely on an absolutely wonderful young woman who looked after our boys (second and fifth grade when we moved to Des Moines) on numerous occasions. And the long-haired clerk at the large electronics store is a composite of some wonderful folks I have encountered in just such a setting. The steep and slippery driveway, quite obviously, is ours at 2907 Terrace Drive.

The huge blizzard described early in the story hit the Chicago area in February 1967 and postponed my participation in the turnabout dance at New Trier High School. Eventually they rescheduled it, and I went with Linda Hughey and had a very nice time. She ended up being one of the first female undergraduates at Yale—very smart about everything except turnabout dates.

"Here and Now"

Part I

Jeff sat by the window and watched the snow falling gently to earth with quiet insistence. He marveled at how his attitude toward snow had changed through the years. He could still remember the excitement he had felt as a child: the chance for snowballs and forts and sledding, the delicious possibility that school would be called off. One year, when he was in high school, a major blizzard delivered him from having to go to a turnabout dance with...what was her name? A huge whiteout closed down the city for the whole weekend and let him off the hook. As he grew still older, snow came to mean skiing.

But today, it just meant disruption and stress. Things were crazy enough with the kids home for the first day of Christmas vacation. But their regular sitter, an older woman, absolutely would not come out in the snow. Jeff had gone into a mild panic until he remembered that Catherine, the college student who kept company with the kids during the summer, would probably be home from school. His phone call woke her up, but she seemed cheerful enough, and ready to help. A few extra dollars just before Christmas couldn't hurt, either. Thank God for the college kid.

Jeff's thoughts of gratitude were short-lived. He heard a sort of rhythmic pounding noise outside, slowly coming closer. In a moment, he realized what it was: the stereo in Catherine's car blasting away. He had heard her before he could see her. She turned into the driveway, wheels spinning valiantly against the snowy incline. Slowly but surely, she made the ascent.

Jeff knew intellectually that people experiment when they go away to college. In fact, he had done his share. But he still wasn't quite prepared for the sight. Catherine had dyed her normally brown hair flaming red. She wore sunglasses and purple lipstick. Once the sunglasses came off, he could see that one eye sported red eye shadow, the other green… very festive. Shredded jeans and a flannel shirt completed the ensemble…almost. He did a double take and tried not to gasp when he noticed that she had had her nose pierced.

"Morning, Mr. Garland," Catherine said. "Sorry I couldn't get here any faster."

"Listen, Catherine," Jeff replied, "I am just thrilled that you could get here at all. I have a very important meeting this morning with some people who are in from out of town. I have a presentation to make, and I'm sure that they will be eager to get out to the airport. You saved my life by coming this early! How are things going for you?"

"Pretty good. I'm glad the semester's over, and I think I did OK. The class I was worried about was organic, but after a while I actually came to enjoy it."

"Organic? You mean chemistry? How come you're taking that?

"I decided on a pre-med major."

"Oh," Jeff said, trying to conceal his surprise. He wondered how Catherine's new look would go over on rounds. "Say, Catherine," he managed diplomatically, "I notice that you have a new image."

"Oh, this," she laughed. "I just don't care how I look."

"I know what you mean," Jeff responded. "When I was in college, we didn't care how we looked, either." But he thought to himself how peculiar it was that everybody managed to dress exactly the same in order to express their freedom from social conformity. The more things change, the more they stay the same.

"Well, Catherine," he said, "I'm off to my meeting. Stevie and Taylor are in the other room. They've already eaten breakfast. I expect to be home between 3:30 and 4 o'clock Muriel won't be back until this evening. Is there anything more I can do before I leave?"

"Just one thing," she replied. "Could you call me 'Cat' from now on? Nobody calls me 'Catherine' except my parents."

"Sure thing," Jeff replied. "See you later, Cat." But once he was out the door, he sighed deeply.

The driving wasn't as bad as he had expected, once he got out onto the main roads. He made it to the office nearly on time, and went directly to the conference room, where he found the folks from the coast dressed for travel, but ready for business. As Jeff took his notes from his briefcase, he reminded himself once again not to seem too eager, not to let his enthusiasm for what he had to say make it seem as though he were carried away by emotion.

He tried to begin slowly. "I am glad we have this opportunity to meet face to face. In order to make this merger the opportunity we all believe it will be, there are some things we will need to attend to. As our organizations come together, we will become the largest company of its kind in North America, and the third largest in the world. There are some tremendous advantages to size, of course. But unless we are careful, there will be some dangerous drawbacks, too. I want to suggest that as our business grows bigger, we will need to become even more attentive to the needs of individual clients.

"People like size. They like the idea of doing business with somebody who will be around tomorrow and the day after.

They like the sense of stability and permanence a large organization offers. And they believe that large enterprises are cost effective. That's the good part.

"But they also mistrust the impersonal. They like people-to-people contact. They have a need to put a face on a big organization." Jeff could see that he had their interest, but he couldn't tell for how long.

"Do you remember when a piece of first-class mail felt like something personal, when just having your name typed on a piece of paper meant that somebody had typed it? Well, no more. With mail-merge capabilities, computers have completely de-personalized first class. Do you even read all your first-class mail anymore?

"And phone calls: Remember when that was a way to reach out? Well, how many of you can make it through dinner every night for a week without being interrupted by a call from AT&T? Or somebody offering you a credit card? And what do you think when that happens: that somebody cares about you? No, you envision a room with 10 million people sitting at phones and calling everybody who has a phone. There's nothing personal in that.

"As we get bigger, we have to find better ways to relate, to protect the customer loyalty that has been the hallmark of both our organizations. And I think I have a plan that will help us do just that. As we grow bigger, we have to grow smaller at the same time."

Jeff was careful not to lose track of time, not to let travel anxiety encroach on his listeners' concentration. When he finished, there was plenty of time for give and take. He sensed that the idea of growing bigger and smaller at the same time made sense to them. A decision was somewhere down the road, but the seed had been planted.

Jeff hopped into his car and drove the now cleared streets toward home, just in time to rescue Cat from the kids... or was it the other way around? And, oh yes: There was the matter of Christmas to attend to.

Part II

This is crazy, Jeff thought to himself. Shopping on Christmas Eve...I've got to be nuts! The secret, of course, was to get started as early as possible, with many of the stores opening by 8 o'clock.

Even without a calendar, he would have known it was Christmas Eve. The oldies station had started in with its Christmas music: "Jingle Bell Rock," "Rockin' Around the Christmas Tree," "Have a Holly Jolly Christmas," and similar cultural treasures for the next 36 hours or so. Jeff switched off the radio to be alone with his thoughts.

Christmas Eve. How did he get into this? He imagined that it must be this way with a lot of couples. Beginning in October, he and Muriel had had endless discussions about the craze for this year: Nintendo 64. They had observed that it's expensive, it sends the wrong message to the kids, it requires all new software, and most of what's available is violent. But finally they caved in. And then, busy people that they were, they both assumed that the matter was over, and neither one of them had actually gone out to buy the thing. Muriel thought Jeff would do it; he thought she would: a classic, "I got it—you take it!" performance...not so unusual.

So here he was on the way to the mall, the last place he wanted to go today. The huge electronics store would have them. Get in, get out.

But it wasn't that easy. The big display of video games looked as though it had been ravaged by the Visigoths. Unwilling to show weakness by asking for directions, Jeff spent a confused couple of minutes looking around, before he saw a small sign that any available Nintendo 64 systems would be sold at the customer service counter. It was off in another corner of the store, about a quarter-mile away.

Behind the counter a number of clerks were doing a random motion routine, moving about aimlessly and managing not to make eye contact with anybody on the other side. They looked busy, but it was impossible to determine what they were doing. At last, Jeff noticed a clerk who was bent over at the waist, hands above (below?) his head grasping his shoulder length hair. In one motion, he straightened up and pulled back his hair, gathering it into a ponytail which he secured with an elastic band with a red-nosed reindeer flashing festively on it. Hair secured, the clerk made the mistake of opening his eyes and looking at Jeff. Contact!

"Man, are you lucky!" he said to Jeff, once the object of Jeff's mission had been revealed. "This is the last one of these in the store. And we wouldn't have this one, except that some people got disgusted and brought it back because they couldn't buy any games for it in time for Christmas...except for the rip-your-heart-out-and-eat-it combat games...can't blame 'em, really, that stuff is pretty gross. But they didn't even wait around long enough for me to tell them that they should just rent some games for the first couple of days, while the thing is still new. In fact, I've got a coupon here good for a free game rental. Do you want it?"

"Gosh," said Jeff, "thanks a lot."

"Hey, no problem," the clerk replied. "I know what it would have meant to me to get something like this for Christmas, and to be able to play with it. I hope your kids have a blast.

Merry Christmas."

Back in the car, Jeff thought, This is just what I was talking about yesterday. What a difference that clerk made in my experience of that place. As huge as it is, my abiding memory will be of that guy with the ponytail who knows how a kid feels at Christmas. What a great experience!

Without thinking, he turned on the radio again. But a few notes of Elvis and "Blue Christmas" had him reaching for the programmed buttons. The first one Muriel had set to National Public Radio. Jeff was surprised to hear the sound of a very British-sounding man reading the Christmas story from Luke. It was part of the traditional lessons and carols service from King's College in Cambridge, England. The reader must have been the headmaster or something like that, for he read with great precision. "And this shall be a sign unto you; Ye shall find the babe wrapped in swaddling clothes, lying in a manger."

The anthem that followed the familiar lesson was a surprise. It was "In the Bleak Midwinter," a hymn Jeff had struggled through in church, but to a different tune. Somehow the unfamiliar melody made the words come through with new clarity, especially when they got to the second verse:

Our God, heaven cannot hold Him, nor earth sustain;

Heaven and earth shall flee away, when he comes to reign;

In the bleak midwinter, a stable place sufficed,
The Lord God almighty, Jesus Christ.

"Wow," Jeff thought to himself. "Talk about being big and overwhelming, but getting small and vulnerable. God, from before time and beyond time, taking human form to be in a relationship with us. God reaching out...by entering in." It was a new thought to Jeff. Something so big, becoming so small to touch human lives. This is not just something God did, but something God does, not just once upon a time, but here and now...here and now.

Part III

Somehow, this Christmas was different. Oh, it was all the same: same rituals, same phone calls to the out of town folks, same food to eat. Maybe that was it. It was all so ordinary, so normal, that he kept tearing up at the oddest moments: the kids ripping into packages like a couple of wild animals, the kids fighting with each other. The very normalcy of it made it seem precious...even the complaining. Same old shirts and ties, familiar—wonderfully familiar—gifts of books and socks and Hershey's kisses.

Cat had stolen the show. She had found an outrageous pair of earrings—the old kind that clip on—at a garage sale someplace and had given one of them to each of the boys. They all got a big laugh out of that. And the tears flowed.

Somehow it was more than a holiday. It was a holy day, because all of these endearingly ordinary things really meant love. To have it come so close and have it mean so much: how did God do that? Creator of the universe...a simple stable...a family gathered...how did God do that?

Usually, it took Jeff a pretty long time to unwind from manic mode on Christmas, to down-shift from making it all happen to letting something happen. But this day was different, and maybe that was the greatest gift of all.

One of his presents, amazingly enough, was a compact disc recording by John Rutter directing the Cambridge singers, and it had that oddly wonderful English version of "In the Bleak Midwinter" on it. The last verse, familiar though it was, caught him by surprise:

> What can I give him, poor as I am?
> If I were a shepherd, I would bring a lamb.
> If I were a Wise Man, I would do my part;
> Yet what I can I give him: give my heart.

1997

I have two older sisters and did my share of pre-Christmas snooping around. The way in which a telephone call can change everything in an instant, and the abrupt role-reversal of parent and child, are things I have seen numerous families go through; although at the time I wrote this, all of that still lay ahead for Priscilla and me with our own parents. The idea of impromptu gatherings in unlikely places hearkens back to the days when Priscilla was in medical school and residency and seldom had holidays off. I have often been deeply moved watching families improvise ways to preserve traditions and express their love. The first Christmas—unexplained pregnancy, no room at the inn, Wise Men going to the wrong place—was an extended exercise in improvisation.

"The Surprise"

Part I

"Quiet," Rebecca whispered to Todd. "I think I hear something." Ordinarily, Todd paid no attention at all to the commands of his older sister. She seemed to think it her solemn responsibility to function as General Superintendent of the Universe, especially with regard to him, and he resented it. But this was a precarious situation, which called for them to depart from the normal Big Sister/Kid Brother script and work together. It was just a few days before Christmas. And with their parents out of the house for a couple of hours—Dad at work and Mom shopping—Rebecca and Todd had taken it upon themselves to do a little "exploring." At 12 and 10 years of age, they had long since discovered all the pre-Christmas hiding places their parents used for the stashing of presents. And parental counterintelligence seemed to be lagging in this crucial area: The old fogies hadn't yet figured out what the kids knew. On other occasions, perhaps when there was more to do or when the kids weren't getting along so well, such an opportunity might have gone unexploited.

But this time, temptation had gotten the better of them.

The noise was cause for concern, all right. It sounded as though somebody was home, but nobody was expected for hours. Katherine, their mother, had headed out for the mall—a place she hated, and consequently didn't know very well...she might never finish out there. And Rick, the dad, had said at breakfast that he had a solid day of meetings and would be late for dinner. The noise was a definite surprise. It sounded like the garage door.

And they had just struck pay dirt. Rebecca had found a suspicious box, which obviously someone had opened and repacked. The cardboard was new. It was not hermetically sealed with tape like the other boxes in the storage area. This was the real thing, all right. But the sounds were getting closer now... a jingling noise like the rustling of keys. Quickly she found it: the packing list she knew would have to be in there somewhere near the top. Her eyes glanced down the list and widened just a moment. Her jaw dropped open. And then a pounding at the door sent her into a frenzy of restoration: list back in the box, box back on the shelf, and the two of them scurrying out of there faster than they had moved in months.

It was, as they knew by now, their mother, Katherine. She was pounding on the door to the garage. "Rebecca!" she called. "Todd! Somebody let me in!" The two conspirators snickered to each other behind their hands. Todd started to move toward the door to let their mother in, but Rebecca restrained him. "Let's savor the moment a bit," she proposed, knowing that she would need every possible instant to collect herself so that her mother, who could read her like a book, would not have her suspicions aroused. At last, when it sounded as though the door were about to open, Rebecca nodded and Todd turned the knob.

"Confounded door keys!" Katherine exclaimed. "They have never worked properly."

"Gosh, Mom," Todd deadpanned. "Nobody else has any problems with that set of keys. Seems to me they work fine."

"Maybe for you, but not for me. I think those door keys should be thrown into the river!"

Todd sensed the opportunity to seize the offense—always the best defense. "Say, Mom, how come you call them 'door keys,' when everybody else just calls them 'keys'?"

"Yeah," Rebecca chimed in. "Don't you think that's kind of dorky?"

That was just too much. Todd completely lost it, and couldn't stop laughing. "Dorky!" he squealed with glee. "Dorky!" He was running around the kitchen, holding his sides, and it took a few moments before he quieted down.

"Say, Mom," Rebecca said, trying to sound casual, "how

come you got home so soon? I thought you were spending our inheritance at the mall."

"Oh," Katherine replied, "it was the traffic. It was absolutely terrible. I got stuck behind a car that was intent on going about 15 miles per hour, and I was getting madder and madder. Then I thought to myself, 'Is this what Christmas is for, for me to have a nervous breakdown sitting in my car?' And I decided that I would just come right back home and finish my shopping over the phone. They can get the stuff here in time for Christmas, and I will have my sanity intact."

Rebecca couldn't resist. "Yeah…what little is left of it. Hey, I'll bet I know who was driving that slow car in front of you. It was some old guy wearing a hat, wasn't it?"

"As a matter of fact it was. But how did you know?"

"They're always the ones that go about 15 miles an hour: old guys with hats. Look out for them!"

Rebecca turned to leave the room. "I will look out for the old guys with hats," Katherine replied. "But you look out for yourself, young lady. Don't be snooping around in strange boxes during the week before Christmas."

Rebecca was speechless. "And don't try to deny it. You know that one of your most endearing qualities is that you are a terrible liar. Don't go ruining any surprises for you or for anybody else. Do you hear me? The surprise is the best part of Christmas."

"Yes, Mother."

That penitential tone to things lasted pretty well into the evening, except for one thing none of them had counted on: the number of times there are jingling bells on radio or TV. Every time that sound was heard, it set Todd off all over again. "Dorky!" he laughed. "Dorky! Ha, ha!"

But all of that was before the phone call.

Part II

Katherine sat in the hospital-like room and reflected on the whirlwind changes a telephone call can bring. At first, the words just flew past her: "Your mother…a stroke…probably not life threatening…speech impairment and some loss of motor abilities…we'll know more in a few days…it would be good if you could come."

It is amazing what suddenly seems inessential in a true emergency. Her mother, Amy, had always been there for Katherine. She was strong, independent, funny—perhaps that more than anything. Ever since her husband's death, Amy had insisted on maintaining her own place. A great believer in the old adage that "Fish and relatives both start to stink after three days," Amy had refused to move closer to Katherine. "My friends are here," she said. "Our lives have been here. We'll still be only three hours apart." The apartment in the retirement complex had seemed just the solution: an infirmary with health care available, meals there if she needed them. Katherine had expected the move to be more traumatic than it was. "Time I got rid of most of this stuff," Amy had said, and that was that. A new place...a new life...let's get on with it. That was her way.

They had talked just a few days earlier. "I'll be relieved when Christmas is over with," Amy had told her daughter. "I feel as though this place is under a state of siege, surrounded by carolers and well-wishers. I wonder where those people will be in the middle of January!" They had laughed together.

Neither of them had expected to spend Christmas Eve in this room in the infirmary. There had been three days in the hospital, while the effects of the stroke were evaluated. But since Amy could swallow on her own, and had no trouble with breathing, the infirmary seemed the answer. Katherine could stay in Amy's apartment, water the plants, and spend the next few days—including Christmas—with her mother. It wasn't Plan A, but it was acceptable under the circumstances.

The staff people were nice enough, considering that they were short-staffed, and all felt at least a little bit abused to be working on Christmas Eve. But now that the crisis had passed, Amy didn't need constant attention from trained professionals. She needed somebody to be there.

And Katherine could do that.

But it was hard to be strong, to be supportive, to be encouraging, when the one who had been her own strength for so long seemed so helpless there in the bed. Katherine had had to struggle with this sudden reversal of roles. Who was the parent now, and who was the child? How many times had Amy done for her the things she was now having to do: help with feeding, and bathing, and even help with speech? Speech was the hardest. Amy's eyes would well up with tears when it was clear that she wanted to say something but couldn't make it happen, this woman who all her life had been so clever with words—painting pictures, eliciting laughter, imparting comfort and support. It seemed somehow as though the words were still all there, but floating around in another dimension; present, yet inaccessible at the same time. Yes, speech was the worst.

The people in the room across the hall had the TV on, and though only part of the dialogue came through, Katherine knew what they were watching. It was the old British version of *A Christmas Carol*, with Alastair Sim as Scrooge. At this particular moment, the Cratchits were once again erupting in Christmas merriment. Tiny Tim, he of the eternal adenoids, was exclaiming once again: "The goose! Oh, Martha, there never was such a goose! And the pudding! Oh, Martha, the pudding!" They had watched it together countless times over the years, and ridiculed the saccharine intimacy it seemed to portray. But they loved it, if only to make fun of. For years, it just wasn't Christmas without *A Christmas Carol.* But tonight it seemed too much. Katherine got up and closed the door just enough to deflect the sound.

Amy moaned. Katherine reached over to touch her cheek. "Mother," she said. "Why don't you just try to sleep? Everything's OK. I'll be here. Sleep is the best thing for now."

Katherine must have dozed off herself for a while. The next thing she knew, the lighting was different in the hallway. The TV was still across the way. The place was silent. But suddenly Katherine was aware that her mother was looking at her. If it is possible to smile just with your eyes, then that is what Amy did. Katherine took her hand.

"I love you, Mother," she said. It was all there was to say. Amy's eyes closed again.

Amy was helpless, just like a baby. This was a whole new dimension to the relationship between mother and daughter. It was odd, yet somehow strangely appropriate at Christmas, when God became a child to reveal a new dimension of love. Sleep, Mother, Katherine thought. Sleep in heavenly peace.

It's OK. You taught me that. Whatever happens, it's OK. I'll be here.

Part III

A possibility that had never occurred to Katherine was the unexpected arrival of the rest of her family. "You stay there," she had said. "There's nothing you can do here, really. Mom just needs some quiet. I'll come home, and we'll do Christmas in a few days." She thought at the time that that argument had carried the day. Wrong!

Katherine had gone up to her mother's apartment to take a shower and have a few moments to herself when there was a plaintive little knock at the door. It was Rick, with Todd, Rebecca, and a whole lot of packages.

"What in the world are you doing here?" Katherine half asked, half exclaimed. "Why aren't you at home on Christmas morning, opening packages?"

"We wanted to be with you and Grandma," Rebecca responded. "We wanted to be together on Christmas."

"Well, I think that's wonderful! And I'm really glad to see you and everything. But I… the stuff I got for you… I haven't had a chance to wrap anything, or…"

"Oh, that's OK, Mom," said Todd. "We wrapped it."

"You wrapped it? You wrapped your own presents?"

"Yeah... well... uh..."

"What he's trying to say," Rebecca chimed in, "is that we knew what we were getting, anyway. We found the box in the attic. You guys are really terrible at hiding stuff. And anyway, we thought that since you wouldn't have a chance to wrap presents, we could wrap them ourselves, so at least somebody would be really surprised when they got opened on Christmas!"

The logic of this failed miserably, of course. But the sincerity of the effort to rescue a family Christmas was unmistakable. Katherine, however, was not about to let the opportunity pass. She reached into her pocket, took out her keys and began to shake them: "Dorky, you guys! Really dorky!"

The day was tough on Amy. But everyone could tell how much it meant to her that Rick and the kids had come, that they were all together on Christmas. And they were together, perhaps even more than they had been during the years when everything went according to plan.

The family was not yet as skilled at attending to Amy's needs as they would become, but they were certainly eager to learn. At one point, Rick was trying to help Amy move in bed, when he lost his grip a bit and his hand slipped. Amy's eyes grew suddenly very wide. Katherine didn't miss a beat.

"Well, Mom, I guess you've had your Christmas goose. There never was such a goose!"

Amy, in characteristic fashion, had done her shopping early, so her gifts were not only purchased, but wrapped and marked. Everybody gasped just a little bit when Rick opened his.

"Gee, Dad," said Todd at last, "nice hat."

"Yeah," added Rebecca. "Now you've arrived. You'll be a stunning profile behind the wheel. Good old Dad, unsafe at any speed."

1998

This is one of my favorite stories, very vivid in my mind. I've always liked this title. I had in mind the Latin saying, *Sic transit Gloria mundi*: "Thus passes the glory of the world." The image of Gloria traveling by bus is irresistible to me as a figure for where God would hang out in our world today. The bus station I envision is the old Continental Trailways station on Route 6 in Grinnell. The counter-melody Gloria sings on "Silent Night" is the "Peace, Peace" introduction the Matins still sing.

"In Transit Gloria"

Part I

Once again, Gloria used the sleeve of her coat to clear a circle of fog away from the bus window. It didn't help much. She peered into the gathering gloom outside, but the encroaching darkness and the blowing snow had reduced visibility to almost nothing. Most of what she could see any more was her own reflection, which revealed a young woman who looked pretty scared.

"You have nobody but yourself to thank for this," she reminded herself for the 1,000th time. When her father had dropped her off at school in the fall, the last thing he had said to her was to be sure to find out when her exams would be done and to make a plane reservation right away for Christmas vacation. But she had to make some changes in her course schedule, and Christmas had seemed an eternity away. One thing led to another, and when at last she realized in a panic that she had no flight arrangements, tickets were just too expensive.

At first, the bus had seemed like an adventure. And the

first day and a half, which got her to Chicago, had gone pretty well. She thought that she would never forget the sight of the sunrise along Interstate 80 in central Pennsylvania. Where was that… Lock Haven? It was gorgeous.

But now that seemed an eternity ago. They had warned passengers in Chicago that the weather would be bad, to travel at their own risk. Many of them had decided to wait it out there. But Gloria and the handful aboard had chosen to plow ahead. How could something as soft and fluffy as snow stop a huge bus like this? She seemed about to find out.

Even for as little as she could see, Gloria had counted more than 50 stranded vehicles. The bus had slowed to a crawl, and she could tell from time to time that the wheels were slipping. What a scary sensation!

"Way to go, Glo," she said to herself. That's what her friends in high school had called her…among other things. Gloria had never liked her name. Gloria Elizabeth. It sounded to her like a tinsel matron, half sleazy movie star and half over-stuffed busybody. Friends, of course, are a big help with such embarrassments. They teased her without mercy, especially at Christmastime. "Hey, Gloria in eggshellsies doo-doo!" they called to her. For a time some of the kids called her GE. But Glo seemed to suit her somehow, though she wasn't glowing too brightly at the moment.

The bus driver interrupted her thoughts. "Friends, as you can tell, we're having some trouble here. There's no way we're going to get through tonight. There's a town up ahead about five miles—a scheduled stop—where we can get off and wait it out. There's a little bus station there. It sounds as though the storm will blow through by morning. If we can get you to some place safe and warm, we can give the road crews a chance to get something done, and try it again at first light. If you're in a hurry to get somewhere, I'm sorry. But nothing is worth getting killed over. At the rate we're going, it'll take maybe 20 minutes to make the five miles."

This turn of events cast a different light on things. When first she had boarded the bus, Gloria had tried not to pay much attention to the handful of other people aboard. She had practiced the urban art of seeing people without really looking at them, avoiding eye contact that might draw her into conversation. Not that she was unfriendly. At school, she had quickly become the one everybody went to with their problems. But on the bus, she had not wanted to become anybody's captive audience for two days. Now she began to wonder about these strangers with whom she would be spending the night.

There was a mother traveling with two children. One of them, Gloria had already learned, was a little boy named

Jordan. She had received this information from Jordan himself, who also told her that he was "this many" years old... four. Jordan seemed to know one verse of one Christmas carol. It was "Away in a Manger," and he could sing it 4,000 times in five minutes. (How had the Guinness people missed this kid?) Jordan's mother seemed to lack the energy to keep up with him. At first she yelled at him to shut up and sit down. But every time she yelled, she was gripped by a bout of coughing, so she quickly resigned herself to letting him have his freedom. He had been to visit Gloria several times. The other child, a daughter, was even younger. She seemed to be sick. Mostly she slept.

Ahead on the right was an older couple. He was wearing a red plaid shirt and one of those plastic mesh baseball caps that all the farmers seem to wear. Gloria tried to guess what was on the front of it. John Deere? Pioneer Hybrid? His wife was wearing a scarf tied tight around her head.

Gloria was also aware that there was someone behind her, a man traveling alone. He was tall, wearing a black stocking cap and headphones. She had noticed him earlier, not only because he looked large and powerful, but because he was carrying one of those big old boom boxes that had been so popular when she was a little kid.

The 20 minutes the driver predicted turned out to be more

like 25. And the so-called bus station was an amazing thing to behold. It was half of a gas station, a room about 10 by 12. The furniture consisted of a single unit. Three green molded plastic chairs were strung together and attached to a corner table, into which was built a lamp; and at right angles, another three green molded plastic chairs (one of them cracked and repaired with gray duct tape) completed the arrangement. It was one of those pieces designed to facilitate cleaning underneath; however, it had been some time since this had provided sufficient inducement to anybody to actually approach it with a broom, let alone a mop. The brown and cream colored linoleum tile was filthy; in areas of heavy traffic, it was worn through down to the concrete.

There were two vending machines, one of which contained candy bars and gum and sported a sign reading, OUT OF ORDER, and the other a coffee and hot chocolate machine. Next to each of the buttons was a light that read, PLEASE MAKE ANOTHER SELECTION.

Well, Gloria thought, one's broken and the other one's empty—the dynamic duo. The pay phone and the unisex restroom were in the gas station half of the building, which seemed to have no heat. It promised to be a very long time until morning.

Part II

The older couple disappeared almost immediately. The little town had been their destination all along. A quick phone call, the appearance of an immense four-wheel-drive pickup, and they were gone before Gloria even realized she'd forgotten to notice what was on the front of his cap.

The bus driver came out OK, too, crossing the street to the only motel in town. But Gloria and the others hadn't counted on the extra expense and settled in to spend the night in the tiny waiting area. At least it was warm.

Gloria surveyed her surroundings more carefully. The useless vending machines were draped with some tired looking tinsel. Hanging on the wall above them were some cutout construction paper letters which once had spelled Happy Holidays in alternating red and green. But now, the I and the D were missing.

The woman with the two children quickly claimed the chairs on one side of the table, leaving Gloria and the man with the stocking cap to sit on the other side with an empty chair between them. He had a duffel bag and the boom box. His face disappeared inside a video game magazine. Above the sound of the snow beating in waves against the window behind her, Gloria could overhear the occasional metallic clash of music from his headphones.

Jordan, of course, was the icebreaker. He had already made contact with Gloria, and immediately set his sights on the man with the stocking cap. He elected the "interpretive dance" approach at first, singing his version of "Away in a Manger" and providing what he took to be appropriate choreography, punctuated with frequent glances to measure the impact on his target. As said impact was minimal at first, Jordan escalated the performance, both in volume and in intensity, until it was impossible to ignore.

At length the man took off his headphones, smiled and said, "Hi. What's your name?"

"My name is Jordan, and I am this many years old [four fingers], and I can sing a song for you: 'Away in a manger, no crib for a bed....'" Jordan managed to get all of that out in one breath, leaving no room for the man to say, "No, thank you."

The man watched the performance and smiled. "That's very nice, Jordan. I like your song."

Jordan was encouraged. "What's your name, and where are you going?"

"My name is Manuel. I have a very long way to go. I am going to Denver to see my uncle for Christmas."

"Do you know any Christmas songs?"

"Sure. Let me sing you one in Spanish." And he began to sing in a surprisingly gentle voice: "*Pastores a Belen, vamos con alegria, porque ha nacido ya, el hijo de Maria.*"

The song was beautiful—haunting, Gloria thought. But Jordan, experiencing spotlight deprivation, quickly lost interest and changed the subject. "Mommy! I'm hungry! Can I have something to eat?"

"No, Jordan. There's nothing to eat here. The best thing you can do is go to sleep."

"I'm hungry! I don't want to go to sleep."

"Shhh. You'll wake your sister. I'm very sorry, but you'll just have to wait."

"Ma'am," said Manuel. "I have a few things in my bag here. I'd be glad to share." He pulled out a box of Twinkies with a smile. "I'm addicted to these things."

Right behind them came a six-pack of Surge. "I suppose this doesn't represent a very balanced diet, but I am glad to share what I have."

"Great," thought Gloria. "Sugar and caffeine: just what Jordan needs." But she had to admit that she was starved, too. So that's where it happened: stranded travelers, thrown together by the storm, shared what they had, and waited for Christmas to come.

Part III

It's funny how these things happen sometimes, but that year the rest of Christmas was anti-climactic for Gloria. Morning had dawned, clear and cold, with the sun shining brightly and the sky a bottomless blue. They were back on the road by 10 o'clock, and soon went their separate ways to their various destinations. But nothing would ever let her forget that night.

After the communion of Twinkies and Surge, Jordan was wired, all right. In self-defense, Gloria decided to teach him a different Christmas carol, and she settled on "Silent Night." Manuel had joined in, along with Jordan's mother, who could sing a little bit when she wasn't coughing. Jordan was a quick learner, and pretty soon he could sing it all the way through. He particularly liked the part where he could slide way up to the high note on "Peeee-eace."

That had given Gloria an idea. She remembered another part that she had learned in choir at church. So once the others were solid on the main melody of "Silent Night," she sang a counter melody about peace on earth: "This is a time for joy, this is a time for love, now let us all sing together of peace, peace, peace on earth."

And that's when Christmas came. That's the funny thing about it. You can never make it happen, but it happens. It comes in the strangest places, at the strangest times, not on cue and according to plan, but wherever people discover and share a love that they know has come to them from beyond. Elsewhere in the world that stormy night, people were working pretty hard at Christmas: making their lists and checking them twice, decking their halls, cooking and baking and worrying about how the family would get along this year. But sometimes all that work makes us miss it.

One year, Christmas came to Gloria in transit. And she'll never be the same.

1999

On numerous occasions, I have walked through the snow to Plymouth in my goggles and ski pants to lead worship with a relative handful of people. Every such instance is memorable. With this story the setting isn't very distinct in my mind, but the people are, and even though the characters are fictitious, I see specific faces as I imagine the conversation. Many of the memories shared are my own.

"Hopes and Fears"

Part I

She's here, all right, Sam thought, almost saying it out loud. The building's warm. She must have walked, and her footprints are already drifted over. Damn fool kid.

In spite of himself, he felt a twinge of pride. As the chair of the search committee, Sam felt largely responsible for bringing the Rev. Karen Brightwell to their little church. Some of the folks thought it was pretty risky calling a woman—divorced, no less—to be the pastor…they'd never had a woman before. But she was clearly the best candidate, and she had been a breath of fresh air for the place. Even though the TV and radio were telling everybody to stay home, somehow Sam knew Karen would be here bright and early. That's just the way she was.

"Hello!" he called out. "Anybody here?" As he expected, Karen came walking in from the sacristy, her hands filled with candles. She was bustling around to get things ready. "Good morning, Sam," she said in a voice that fairly sang. She grinned as she said, "I might have known you'd be foolish enough to be here."

"Well, you know," he said gruffly, "I spent all that money on that four-wheel-drive gas-guzzler, so I thought I'd try it out. Besides, I figured you'd be here, and you'd need a ride home. Is it just you and me?"

"So far. Tons of people have called in to see if we're still having a service. I told them that of course the children's program is canceled. Everybody's real disappointed about that, but even more relieved that they don't have to come out. I've told people that I'll be here in case anybody shows up, but they should stay home with a clear conscience. From what they say, it's pretty dangerous out there. It was beautiful as I walked over, but I wore my ski bibs and goggles. I'll bet it was easier to walk than to drive. It still took me about half an hour to cover the half a mile. Pretty strange for the Sunday before Christmas!"

"I don't know if much of anybody will come out," Sam said. "I think most of them have more sense that we do. Anything I can do to help?"

"Well, I thought I would put out some fresh candles. Even if we don't use them today, we can use them for Christmas Eve."

"Good enough. I'll give you a hand."

Together, they busied themselves with putting out the candles that would transform the tiny sanctuary for Christmas. The wind continued to howl outside. The young pastor sang as she worked: "O come, all ye faithful, joyful and triumphant...." Sam, who couldn't carry a tune in a bucket, hummed silently to himself.

They were nearly finished when they heard a strange scraping noise outside. It lasted for two or three minutes and was punctuated at the end by the appearance of Robin James, the president of the church's youth group. He appeared, red-faced and sweating, his uncovered head flocked with snow. "Man!" he exclaimed, "is it ever blowing out there! It was our day to clear the walks, but I don't think we're going to get it done. I hardly made a dent!"

"Good grief, Robin!" Karen said. "Didn't you hear the radio and TV? They're telling everybody to stay home."

"Really? I was the first one up at our house, and I just headed out. I could tell it was bad, but I didn't know it was this bad. Are we the only ones here?"

"That seems to be the case," said Sam. "Just the three of us."

No sooner had he spoken than the door opened and a red-haired woman sputtered in. "Let's get going!" she said. "Nobody else at my house would come out. But I've been planning this Christmas all year, and this service is a part of it. I think we should begin."

"Well, I don't know, Harriet," Karen said, "I've got some coffee made and there are some cookies in the fridge, so at least the coffee hour's taken care of. But we were planning on a children's program today. Obviously, that isn't going to happen. But I suppose we could at least read the lessons. You know: wherever two or three are gathered."

"Precisely," Harriet agreed. "Let's get on with it."

The reading of the lessons took about five minutes. There

were four lessons and four people, so each one read one: Old Testament, New Testament, Epistle, Gospel. Then they just looked at each other.

"I have an idea," Karen proposed. "Since nothing else is prepared for today, why don't we all sort of do the sermon together? Can you think of a memory of Christmas that you'd be willing to share, some Christmas that was either especially good or especially bad, but that for some reason is really memorable? Let's just think about that for a moment, and then I'll begin."

Part II

The sharing was surprisingly easy, once they got going. Karen told about a painful recent Christmas when, between Christmas and New Year's, she came home from a friend's house to find her parents already dismantling the tree and throwing away the ornaments. They were getting ready to move into a condo, and it was as though they couldn't wait to be done with everything having to do with the past. "I felt as though they were throwing away my childhood," she said. "It was awful."

Robin went next. "I had a really weird Christmas about three years ago," he said. "You know that my sisters are older than I am, so in recent years they like to sleep in on Christmas morning. One of them even wants to open all the presents on Christmas Eve. Can you imagine that? Well, a few years ago, when I was in about seventh grade, I woke up all by myself on Christmas morning. I waited around for a while, but it got to be nearly 8 o'clock and I was still the only one up, and I just couldn't stand it any more, so I started to open my presents all by myself. I got all this really cool stuff. A fishing rod and a tennis racket. My folks had even gotten me a set of used golf clubs, and they wrapped them in this big white sheet and decorated it like a snowman. It was really neat to be getting all these things I liked, and I went tearing into that stuff. You should have seen the wrapping paper fly! But then in a minute it was all over. At first I was really happy, but then I felt sort of empty. It would have been a lot more fun to have everybody there. Doing it all by myself sort of ruined it. It was weird."

"The sharing is a big part of it, isn't it?" said Karen.

"Yeah. It really is."

Sam went next. "The Christmas I will never forget was the one where we had everybody together—when our son Jim was still alive. You remember that he was killed in an accident... gosh, it's nearly 25 years ago now. But the last Christmas he was with us was really special, and the strange thing was that everybody knew it was special, too. Everybody got along really great, and nobody got bent out of shape about anything. I don't know what it was about that one. We did the same things we always did. But it all went just great. We never dreamed it would be the last one we'd all have together. Every year since, I have thought about that Christmas. For a long time, I was angry that so much had been taken from us. But as the years go by, I find myself more and more grateful that we ever had it at all."

They were silent together for a long time. Finally Harriet said, "I guess it's my turn. Whenever I think of Christmas, I think of my father. He was not around very much while I was growing up. He was a salesman, and he traveled a lot, and when he was home he was often very tired. He was rather impatient with the noise and commotion children create; consequently, I experienced him as distant and aloof. But Christmas was always different. It seemed to be the only time of the year when he really relaxed, and I remember him as being very affectionate. He read to us. When we were young, it was always Clement Moore's "A Visit from St. Nicholas," the poem most people know as "'Twas the Night Before Christmas." He would read so expressively! It was just wonderful! He just made St. Nicholas come alive for us!

And later on, as we grew older, he would read from

Charles Dickens' *A Christmas Carol.* People always say that Alistair Sim, the British actor, was the definitive Scrooge. But that is only because they never heard my father read the part! We were never wealthy, and some Christmases the only gifts we got would be an orange, some candy, a pair of socks or a sweater. But I never felt as close to my father as I did at Christmas!"

The four of them sat together for a few meaningful moments. Then Karen decided to take a chance. "How about this Christmas?" she asked. "How are you doing today? Who would like to begin?"

Surprisingly, it was Robin who chimed in first. "I used to always look forward to Christmas; but this year, I don't know. Whenever we all get together, my mother seems to be really uptight. She starts to drink a lot, and she yells at everybody. At first, everything is OK, and everybody's really glad to see everybody. But usually something sets it off and things get tense. I've noticed that my sisters tend to make other plans. They might be home for a couple of days, but no more than that. Any more, I'm glad when it's over. People get weird at Christmas."

Nobody knew what to say for a moment. Then it was Harriet who responded. "I think I know what you mean, Robin," she said, "because I think I must be one of the people, who, as you put it, 'get weird.' I have realized that my determination to have the perfect Christmas must be quite a burden to the rest of the family, as though a perfect Christmas would bring us all together. After all, much of it is like today's weather: There isn't a lot I can do to control it. No matter how much I plan, how hard I work on the decorations or the meal or the gifts, those really aren't the things that bring us together. And sometimes I spend so much time working at Christmas that I fail really to share it with my family. Thank you, Robin. It must have been hard for you to share that, but it has helped me."

Sam went next. "I am feeling pretty good about Christmas this year. It was just pretty tough for a lot of years, but now it's OK. The grandchildren are a heck of a lot of fun, and it seems as if it's something different every year. Our kids have gotten to be pretty good company as they have grown older. They'll all be here. Jenny seems to have things under control. I'll help out wherever she lets me. It'll be good. The thing I feel really good about this year is what's happening at the church. Karen, I just think you've brought us a lot of energy around here. I'm sorry the children's program didn't happen today; as you know, it has been a few years since we had one. But I am sure looking forward to Christmas Eve."

"Thank you, Sam," Karen said, as she reached out and

squeezed his arm. "That means a lot to me. You folks have really welcomed me not just into your church, but into your lives, and into your hearts. When I was a kid, I was a real Christmas freak. I would count down the days to Christmas, and I thought it would never come. I would look through my underwear drawer, and count the days, and figure out which pair would be my Christmas underwear. Time just crept along. And now it just flies! The challenge is to find moments to savor, some time when I can just be completely present, without running through a mental checklist or planning the next event. Today has been very special for me. This snowstorm has been a gift, and so have you."

They said a prayer together, and Karen began to sing again: "It came upon the midnight clear, that glorious song of old." Each joined in, in his or her own way.

Part III

The little church was packed on Christmas Eve. "Rescheduling the children's program was exactly the right thing to do," Karen thought. True, some families had left town. But there were other children who were visiting relatives in the congregation, and their families had been more than willing to get them out from underfoot long enough to practice for the program. Two extra rehearsals had helped a lot. They were ready.

They began with a carol sing, all the favorites: "Joy to the World," "Hark! The Herald Angels Sing," "Angels We Have Heard on High." But it was "O Little Town of Bethlehem" that took Karen by surprise. "The hopes and fears of all the years are met in thee tonight," she sang, and as she did she happened to look up and meet Harriet's eyes... and Sam's... and Robin was looking at her, too. Hopes and fears, memories and tears, laughter and joy: it was all there, the room filled to overflowing with all the stuff of life which God, as a child in a manger, came to share. Every heart full to overflowing... every life with a story, a whole host of stories, about the meaning of love and family and life.

If only there were some way we could share what this means to everybody. If only we could open our hearts to one another, to life, to God, to the world. "We hear the Christmas angels the great, glad tidings tell; O come to us, abide with us, our Lord, Emmanuel." "The hopes and fears of all the years are met in thee tonight."

As Karen brushed away a tear, the children—unpredictable as ever in the garb of angels, shepherds and the rest—flocked erratically to the front of the church to tell the story of Christmas.

2000

Of all the stories I have written, my deepest emotional connection is to this one. It recounts, in slightly veiled form, an incident we had gone through with one of our sons the previous year just before Christmas. Many of the details are changed, but the feelings are right as nearly as I can remember them, and those memories are still quite vivid. The word "angel" simply means "messenger." I am struck by how often we become messengers of God, angels, to one another. When the mother in the story says, "Just bring us some good news," she speaks for us all. Christmas is the visitation of joy—glad tidings of great joy—upon shepherds who are terrified by the abrupt arrival of angels. The chaplain described here is a real person, and he was just such an angel in our lives.

"Angel's Song"

Part I

John briefly lost his balance as he reached down to take off his right sock. Just another reminder of getting older, he thought to himself. I used to be able to balance on one foot all day. He leaned against the wall to get the left one off, and slid into his slippers.

It had been a lovely evening, crisp and cold. The snow that had fallen earlier in the day had now been cleared away, and the stars were all out. It was amazing how a little bit of snow helped things feel like Christmas. Earlier, the neighbors' Christmas lights and decorations had seemed like loud people at a party, just trying too hard. But suddenly the lights were just right: radiant, festive, fun. Snow didn't help the driving, but it sure made everything look great.

Thus inspired, John and Sheila had proceeded to check off a couple more annual rituals. They got out their tape of *A Christmas Carol*—the George C. Scott version Sheila favored—put a log on the fire and had some eggnog. Now with the prospect of getting to sleep at a decent hour—something they swore every morning that they would do and seldom accomplished—John was in high spirits as he prepared for bed.

He was brushing his teeth when the phone rang. His first thought was that it was probably for their son, Richard, the 16-year-old target of most calls to their household. But Richard was out for the evening, enjoying the first freedom of Christmas break; he wouldn't be home until midnight. His friends, as if by ESP, rarely called when he was gone. John paused for a moment, holding his breath, trying to decide whether to spit and dash for the phone. But the ringing stopped. Sheila had it.

He listened long enough to try to figure out who was calling. It sounded as though Sheila was in management mode: terse replies, gathering information. "Yes, I see. Where is he? How long ago?"

John decided it must be somebody from work, so he went back to the pressing matter of oral hygiene. As he finished, he looked up into the mirror and saw that Sheila was standing behind him. Their eyes met. He saw the fear right away.

"It's Richard. He's been in an accident. He's at the hospital."

"Is he hurt?"

"They wouldn't say much… just that we should come. I'll go and you can stay with Amy." But again it was her eyes, this time telling him that maybe that wasn't the best idea. He turned to face his wife.

"Let's both go. The Thompsons are home next door. I'll bet Rachel would be glad to stay here in case Amy wakes up. She'll be all right."

As Sheila drove to the hospital, there was little they found to say. The whole range of possibilities flashed through their minds. She was making a conscious effort, John could tell, not to drive too fast. As they drove he looked around at the Christmas decorations and wondered whether, for the rest of his life, they would have the power to bring back this moment, with its strange emptiness and fear.

The emergency room people were all they should be: calm and caring. It's strange how one person's crisis of a lifetime can be part of another's daily routine. "You will be able to see your son in just a few minutes," the receptionist said. "While you're waiting, we need some information." All the crucial data were assembled, securing identity and assuring payment. John noticed for the first time the closeness between the words "numbness" and "numbers."

A man in green scrubs approached. "Are you Richard's parents? You can come on back for just a moment. They brought him in about half an hour ago. It was a single car accident. Apparently he hit some ice and skidded sideways into a pole. He has not been conscious. His vital signs are stable, but we can tell he has received a blow to the head. We're not certain about other injuries. We have some tests to run, and we're going to be pretty busy with him for a while here. If you want to just take a look for a moment or two, that will be fine."

As they followed through the door and down the hall, John and Sheila tried to prepare themselves for what they might see. It was a very small room. Apart from what was attached to the walls and the ceiling, everything was on wheels, lending a sense of transient urgency. Richard lay on a gurney, eyes closed, surrounded by a swarm of people who were conversing in code and oblivious to the arrival of outsiders.

"These are the parents," their docent said to the assembled group. A woman who seemed to be in charge was gentle but all business. "We don't have a lot to tell you right now. We're concerned about head trauma. We're trying to check everything else out. Please just be a moment."

Sheila reached out to touch her son's arm. "Richard," she said. "It's Mom. You're at the hospital. You've been in an accident, and everything's going to be just fine. Dad and I are here. You're going to be OK." The wishful words seemed to hang in the air, surreal, powerless to penetrate the mayhem. Richard showed no response. John stepped forward and reached out to touch his son's head. How soft his hair felt, how helpless he seemed. Rocking chairs…late night feedings…quiet assurance from father to son: somehow all of this was a part of the moment, too. "Hang in there, son," he said. "We're here."

Now the man who had guided them back again took charge: "The waiting room is just down the way and across the hall. There's a phone in there, in case you need to call someone. We'll keep you posted as things develop. Is there anything I can get for you?"

They glanced at each other. "Nothing we can think of," Sheila replied. "Just bring us some good news."

"We're doing everything we can."

"Of course you are. Thank you for your kindness."

In the waiting room, John and Sheila looked at one another, trying to get their bearings and decide what to do next. A man in a clerical collar approached them.

"Are you Richard's parents? My name is Larry. I am the chaplain on call tonight, and I'll be here all night long if you need anything."

John looked him over, not seeing much: a rumpled looking man in soft shoes, carrying a few extra pounds. Great! John thought. A useless, hovering person for us to take care of. If I try to talk to this guy, I'm going to come apart at the seams.

"Thank you very much," he heard himself say. "I think we're just going to have to wait for some news. Our son's been in an accident, and they're trying to figure out how badly he's hurt. We'll just have to wait it out."

Larry nodded. "If there's anything you need, here's my pager number. I'll try to keep tabs on things for you. It's hard to say how quickly things will develop, but I'll check in from time to time to let you know what's happening."

"That will be fine," John said. He expected very little.

Part II

Time passed slowly. John and Sheila called home to see how their neighbor Rachel was doing with Amy. She assured them that Amy had not woken up, that things were fine at home, that they should do whatever they needed to do at the hospital and not to worry. That was a relief. They deliberated about calling the grandparents but decided against it, since they didn't know what in the world to say. So they sat.

From time to time, they reflected on what was happening: how Richard had looked so peaceful, the doctors and nurses were so professional. But every once in awhile, the enormity of their fear would revisit them, and they would hug and cry, just holding on for dear life—literally, for dear life.

Each in their own way, they prayed: at first just the quick and automatic, "Oh, God..." kind of prayer, with no words and little formed thought. As the night wore on, though, content came: prayers for Richard's recovery, of course...thanks for the skill and training of the medical people...gratitude for the gift their son had been in their lives...thanks that nobody else had been hurt. Then more tears and hugs, hugs and tears.

The amazing thing was Chaplain Larry, who had this uncanny knack of showing up at the right moment. First it was coffee: He found it and made it. Then he produced some pillows and a blanket, astoundingly useful for a chaplain. And at every step, he kept them informed. "Now they're doing an EEG...no signs of internal bleeding...the chief concern right now is swelling around the brain...they are thinking about moving him to pediatric intensive care... the next three hours should tell the tale."

He came to get them when it was time to move, and he was actually a part of the team: adjusting the IV tree on the side of the gurney, helping the orderly push the unwieldy thing, clearing the way to the elevator, motioning to John and Sheila where to stand as they rode together to the intensive-care floor.

The pediatric ICU was a strange blend of technology and Walt Disney. Little things struggled to make it a more kid-friendly place: a Christmas tree in the corner, cartoon characters adorning the walls, lights around doorways and at the nurses' station. These efforts were not altogether successful, but they showed that somebody cared, and that mattered a great deal.

John and Sheila had the waiting room to themselves for a while. Then a very anxious-looking man in his 20s came into the room and strode to the TV. Brandishing the remote like a gun he ran through the channels at a dizzying pace. Infomercials for insomniacs flew by, rotisseries and ab machines and psychics, real estate and hot babes and George Foreman blurring together, round and round and round. Then abruptly, he tossed the remote on a couch, clutched at a shirt pocket for a package of cigarettes and left the room as suddenly as he had come, all without a word.

He had left the TV on, tuned to the public channel and a rerun of some long ago Christmas program from England. A very academic personage was reading the Christmas story from Luke, when Chaplain Larry returned, this time accompanied by a doctor.

"And there were in the same country shepherds, abiding in the field, keeping watch over their flock by night…."

"This is Dr. Koslinski," Larry said. "These are Richard's parents, John and Sheila."

"And the angel said unto them, 'Fear not: for behold, I bring you...'"

"It's nice to meet you both. I have some pretty good news for you. As you know, we have been concerned about potential swelling around Richard's brain...."

"For unto you is born this day in the city of David a Savior..."

"But I think that by now, the crisis has passed. We're going to want to keep Richard in intensive care for a while, probably at least until this afternoon, so that we can monitor him closely. Then, if things continue to improve, we ought to be able to move him to a regular floor...."

"And it came to pass, as the angels were gone away from them into heaven, the shepherds said one to another, Let us now go even unto Bethlehem..."

"With a bit of luck, he could go home in a couple of days. Head trauma can be tricky. We will want to watch him for signs of brain damage; but at this point, things look very good—much better than we might have expected. I am hopeful that he will be all right."

"And all they that heard it wondered at those things which were told them by the shepherds. But Mary kept all these things, and pondered them in her heart...."

"Thank you, Doctor, thank you!" Sheila said. "May we see him now?"

"Yes. You may see him for a little while. If you like, you may sit with him in his room. But what he most needs now is rest. I'll check back with you in the morning."

Part III

It was more than they ever expected: the family gathered around the table again. There had been some lonely and anxious nights. Every time the phone would ring around 10 o'clock, John and Sheila felt a wave of dread. Amy had really been shaken by the thought of losing her brother and gave him a huge hug when he came home from the hospital. The smallest thing made everybody cry.

But they were so grateful. All the trappings of Christmas seemed both wonderfully precious and utterly unnecessary: precious because they were sharing them—cherished traditions that were so much a part of their lives and their love; unnecessary because it was so clear that this year it very nearly came to mean nothing.

Now, with table spread and candles lit, they knew that they were sharing a moment they would never forget.

"Let's go around and share what we're thankful for," said John. "I know that's something we usually do at Thanksgiving, but today feels like Thanksgiving, and I'd like to hear from everybody. Richard, would you start?"

"I'm just grateful to be alive. I can't believe how stupid I feel, how close I came to killing myself in that car. I am happy to be here."

Amy was next. "I am glad my brother is here. None of the rest of it means anything without being together." Then she got a puckish grin on her face and said, "Besides, he's the only one who knew where he hid my Christmas present!"

Now it was Sheila's turn. "My heart goes out to everyone who has ever suffered a loss at Christmastime. I know it's tough whenever, but I think Christmas is especially hard. I think we have learned a very important lesson about what matters."

John was very quiet. "I am grateful for the sense that God is with us. I felt God's presence very strongly at the hospital, especially whenever that strange rumpled chaplain kept showing up, and I feel it right now. I am more grateful than words can say that things turned out the way they did for us. I know it could have been otherwise. But I also think I learned that somehow nothing could ever overcome the love we have for each other, or the love God has for us. That's what this means to me." Then through his tears he managed, "Merry Christmas, everybody! Let's eat!"

2001

I don't remember what got me started with "Silent Night" this year, but the website was just as described. The world of middle school and reports was very familiar at the time. I vaguely recall that, after the emotional intensity of the previous year's story, I was looking for something a bit lighter in tone. Obviously in that sense, this story itself turned out to be a Plan B—much more intense than I expected.

The account of a family in grief, though familiar to me in many respects, was not based on anyone in particular. The Festival Service of Nine Lessons and Carols broadcast on the morning of Christmas Eve from King's College in Cambridge, England, is an annual Christmas observance at our house and figures prominently in a number of the stories. They, too, have a website, from which you can download and print a program for the service which includes all the prayers and readings and the words to all the anthems.

"The Plan B Carol"

Part I

"The story of 'Silent Night,' by Ellie Holbert," she began.

Ellie was too nervous to risk eye contact with any of the other students, so she just read from her written report. "'Silent Night' is the world's favorite Christmas carol, but we wouldn't have it at all if everything hadn't gone wrong one Christmas Eve in Austria."

With this dramatic statement, she ventured a look around, hoping her words had connected with her classmates. But middle school is middle school, and the last day before winter vacation is not the day to make an oral report in homeroom. For three days now, class members had been listening to one another offer presentations on various customs relative to the holidays. At first, they were very polite to the speakers, reasoning that if they were attentive when others spoke, they might be treated kindly in return. But Ellie was last, and the peace on earth and goodwill were all long since used up. She did the only thing she could do, and plowed ahead.

"The year was 1818. Father Joseph Mohr was the priest at the St. Nicholas Church in the little mountain town of

Oberndorf, Austria. He always loved Christmas a lot and was really looking forward to the Christmas Eve service at St. Nicholas Church. Soon the day would be here.

"But then a terrible thing happened. Franz Gruber, the church organist, sat down to practice for the special service. But the organ wouldn't work. He went to check it out and discovered that mice had eaten a hole in the belows of the organ."

Mrs. Kennedy the teacher interrupted: "Excuse me, Ellie. Did you say, 'belows'"?

"Yes, ma'am."

"Perhaps were you thinking of 'bellows'? The bellows of an organ move the air that blows through the pipes to make the music."

"'Bellows'... yes, that's probably right. Thank you."

"Ellie, you may continue as soon as the class is quiet... and I'm not going to tell you again. Who wants to go to the office?" Several class members snickered and pretended to raise their hands, but Mrs. Kennedy ignored them. "Ellie, please continue."

"He went to check it out and discovered that mice had eaten a hole in the bellows of the organ. And this was before duct tape was even invented."

Ellie looked around hopefully to see if anybody was laughing at the lame joke her father had insisted she add to the speech…blank stares. She decided to pick up the pace a little bit. "'What will we do?' Gruber said. 'The organ isn't working, and Christmas Eve is today. There won't be any music for the service tonight.' Father Mohr said, 'I know what. I can play the guitar. Let's write some Christmas music that we can do with the guitar.'

"So they worked together. Joseph Mohr wrote the words, and Franz Gruber wrote the music. They came up with 'Silent Night,' except that it was in German first before it was translated into English. It was really pretty, and everybody liked it. Now we sing it all over the world. But it wouldn't have happened at all if the organ hadn't broken down. The end."

Ellie moved quickly toward her seat. But Mrs. Kennedy stopped her: "Ellie, please stay up front to see if there are any questions."

Evan Richards had one: "So you're saying that 'Silent Night' should be played on guitar? Kind of a heavy metal sound?"

Everybody laughed. Mrs. Kennedy intervened: "Are there any serious questions for Ellie?"

Janelle Brown said, "Are you trying to tell us that 'Silent Night' was like a mistake, that it shouldn't have happened at all? Because I think I agree with you!"

"Not exactly," Ellie said. "It's a good thing that happened because something else went wrong. It's like when Columbus wanted to sail to India and ended up discovering America by mistake. It wasn't what he wanted in the first place, but it turned into something good. If the organ in that church had been working, we'd never have had 'Silent Night.'"

Part II

Three candles on the Advent wreath lent a warm glow to the room as the Holberts gathered for dinner that evening. They needed all the warmth and glow they could get. Things had moved so quickly: in February, the horrible headaches; in March, the diagnosis of a fast-growing brain tumor. There was nothing they could do. Within a few weeks, the symptoms began to intensify: sudden changes in personality, then loss of control of her body. Karen Holbert died near the end of August, leaving her husband, Greg, and children, Kevin and Ellie, to fend for themselves.

It wasn't easy. Christmas was especially hard, getting out all the things they had packed away last year, back before the long nightmare began. But they did the best they could, keeping some of their traditions alive, lighting candles against the darkness, trying to hold one another together. Some evenings at dinner, though, conversation was hard to come by.

"Oh, Ellie!" Greg remembered to ask his daughter at last. "How did that report go at school?"

"OK."

"Well, did the other kids seem interested in it?"

"Sort of."

"Did they say anything?"

"Not really. Mostly they were just interested in vacation starting."

"Yeah, I'll bet. You sure drew the short straw in having to go last. Did they laugh at the duct tape line?"

"No, Dad."

"Some people's children simply don't appreciate the finer things of life!"

Finally Kevin joined the conversation: "What was your report about, squirt?"

"'Silent Night.'"

"Yeah? What about it?"

"I told them about how it was written for guitar because the church organ broke down on Christmas Eve when mice ate a hole in it."

"Oh, that stupid old story! That's a crock! It comes from a children's book we have upstairs someplace. Somebody made it up so they could make it into a Disney cartoon in the '60s or something. You don't believe that, do you?"

"What do you mean? I read it in..."

"Oh, yeah! Like it's true because somebody wrote it down? Let's just find out about 'Silent Night.'"

Suddenly a man on a mission, Kevin got up from the table and moved the few steps to the computer. Within a couple of minutes he had it in front of him: the Silent Night Museum website, with biographies of Joseph Mohr and Franz Gruber, pictures of where they had grown up, a link to a picture of the oldest known manuscript of "Silent Night" in Mohr's own hand, and a nasty electronic version of how "Silent Night" probably sounded in its earliest arrangement. "Look at this!" Kevin shouted in triumph. Eagerly, he read aloud:

"'In a 1967 book, there is a silly tale of mice eating the organ bellows (easily repaired). After a great deal of research, most historians feel that Father Mohr, due to his love of guitar music, simply wanted a Christmas song that he could play on his guitar...The story is simple and needs no embellishment. Joseph Mohr wrote the poem in 1816 and Franz Gruber wrote the music on Christmas Eve in 1818.'

"You told that stupid story about the mice in a school report? I swear, Ellie, you'll believe anything!"

Ellie just sat there with her head down, taking it, tears welling up in her eyes. When she spoke at last, in her voice was more hurt and loss than anger: "Kevin, why do you have to be so horrible? Ever since Mom died, you've just been mean."

Quietly, she got up and left the room.

It was at least a couple of minutes before Greg spoke to his son. "Kevin," he said, "you've got to cut the kid some slack. You're four years older. You live in a different world."

"I fail to understand how letting her believe in stupid stories will help her adjust to the real world. Dad, sometimes bad things happen and nothing good comes from them at all. Nothing." With that Kevin, too, left the room, leaving Greg alone with his thoughts and the faint glow of the candles. "God, this is hard!" he thought. "This is just so hard." Then he got up to find and comfort his daughter.

Part III

It was hard, but he felt he had to do it. For years, Greg and Karen had always listened on the radio to the Christmas Eve Service from King's College in Cambridge, England. It was on in the morning—early evening in England—and it seemed to get their Christmas Eve started right. Some years they were busy with last-minute shopping, some years they were cooking, some years they were even in the car to spend

Christmas with relatives. But almost always they listened at least to a part of it.

Each year, it was a blend of the familiar and the new. The lessons were always the same: nine readings beginning in Genesis and moving through the prophets and into the gospels to tell the story of the anticipation and the arrival of Jesus, the Word made flesh. The accents always sounded a bit stuffy, the traditional language of the King James Version a bit stilted and Shakespearean. But the music, both old and new, was flawlessly performed. Some years were better than others, but every year was worth the effort to listen. Even in years when they weren't physically together, listening was something they could share.

As Greg listened by himself, at first the loneliness of it all was overwhelming. But then he began to hear in the service things he'd never paid attention to before: the early prayers remembering "those who mourn…." Never had he imagined that he would be among them. And then there was the prayer for those "who rejoice with us, but upon another shore and in a greater light." The thought of Karen rejoicing hadn't really occurred to him before. The thought that she might be experiencing Christmas in a wonderful new way was a startling idea that would take some getting used to. But somehow, it was comforting.

The first lessons swept by, and a flood of memories with them: times and places—in the car, in the kitchen, wrapping presents when the children were still little. He experienced it all over again.

But as the service turned from Genesis and Old Testament prophecy to the more familiar Christmas stories, Greg was struck by something he had never noticed before: The whole thing was a disaster, really. If the idea was that God's Plan A had Adam and Eve living happily every after in blissful obedience, then things went haywire from the get-go. And somehow all of it, and all of us, amounted to nothing less that a long journey back home. Maybe that was the point.

And the Christmas story itself…what a mess! A young, unmarried girl turns up pregnant with a story that God did it. A Roman census sends her scurrying with her fiancé/husband over the mountains on a donkey. There is no room at the inn. Shepherds, upon receiving glad tidings of great joy, are frightened out of their wits. Wise men come to the wrong place—Jerusalem, not Bethlehem—because it turns out that the baby king is not in the capital but in some backwater town in the hills.

What sense does this story make, really? Who would draw it up this way? Who, indeed?

Greg was so lost in thought that he almost didn't notice

Kevin enter the room and sit down next to him on the couch. As Greg looked up to greet his son, Kevin said to him, "Are you listening to this thing again? How can you stand it? God, I miss Mom!"

"Me, too, Kevin. Me, too," Greg said as he reached out for his son. They hugged and cried together. "Kevin, it hurts like crazy. Sometimes I think I'm going to go nuts. It will never be the same. But you know what? It's going to be all right. It is. I think Mom's OK, and she wants us to be OK, too. Don't you feel that?"

"Sure I do, Dad. It's just that I don't know what OK will feel like. I can't even imagine it."

"Neither can I really, Kev. But I believe in it. I know it works out that way. A lot of times good things show up in the strangest places. Even here. I think that's what Christmas is all about, really. Even here."

"I hope you're right, Dad. God, I hope you're right."

They sat together for a few minutes, listening to the reading from John about the Word made flesh. Then the choir began simply, quietly, to sing in German: "*Stille Nacht, heilege Nacht*!" Kevin turned toward his father and said, "I think I need to have a talk with Ellie."

2002

For many years, I've found it ironic that couples who become empty nesters often add onto their homes in some way. I suppose this is very Iowan: If we build it, they will come. But the concept of space designed for hospitality is a compelling counterpoint to a story in which there is no room at the inn.

"The Guest Room"

Part I

"So, do we have a deal?" Jennifer's voice had that edge to it, the special intonation that told Steve he'd better pay attention. Grateful for the distraction of driving, he kept his eyes on the road and tried to play innocent.

"A deal about what, dear?"

"You know very well what. About the room. Do you promise me that you're not going to say anything about the room?"

Despite himself, Steve was struck by the injustice of the gag order. "Oh, come on! As if I'm ever the one who brings it up. It's your dad who always wants to rub our noses in it. First it was pouring over the plans, then the 1,000-page catalog of hinges, doorknobs and drawer pulls, then paint samples and wallpaper swatches. The man just won't let it alone. And the website! Follow the building progress day by day! That's way over the top! And your father doesn't know anything about computers! How in the world did he come up with a website?"

"I told you, it was Jim's girl—who, as you may recall happens to be your niece, Angela.

"Remember? She's taking classes at the community college. She did all the web stuff, and she even found a program that helps them plan how the room will be decorated and the furniture arranged. She's actually been a big help. Sound familiar?"

Steve did remember now. Jennifer continued, "It's been a good thing for Angela to have all that contact with her grandparents. That girl has just been out of control."

"You can say that again," Steve agreed. "What color is her hair this week, purple? More body piercings than the goalie on the dart team. And I can only imagine the tattoos. It almost makes me glad not to have kids. But you'd think that Jim and Karen would catch on: The tighter they clamp down, the more Angela rebels. God only knows what she'll do for an encore. Is she going to be there tonight?"

"Last I heard, Jim, Karen and Angela are all going to be there. That's why I need you on your best behavior." There was that tone again. "Do I have your word?"

"Oh, I suppose so. But isn't it just the dumbest thing you ever heard of?" He was off again, and she just let him go. "Your folks live all those years in that little house, raise your brother and you there, you two finally grow up and move out, and now, retiring at 70, when they should be relaxing and simplifying their lives, they decide to add onto the house. I tell you, it makes no sense!"

"Steve, I know exactly how you feel about it. You've told me 1,000 times. And Dad and Mom know how you feel about it, too. You've made your point over and over. But it's their lives, it's their money, it's their business. I don't want to ruin Christmas with another conversation about the addition. Let them have their fun, and keep your opinions to yourself."

Despite himself, Steve was heating up. "Fun? Fun?! Fun, I understand. Fun is a trip to Tahiti. This is just a remarkable waste of resources and energy. But you're right. I'm not going to bring it up. We'll just have a nice family dinner. It will be good to see everybody again."

"Promise?"

"Yes, I promise."

But neither of them was quite prepared for the sight that awaited. They made the familiar turns into the familiar neighborhood and negotiated the final right turn onto the street where Jennifer's parents lived. From nearly a block away, they could see it: the addition sticking out from the side of the formerly modest home. It was awash in light from three powerful spotlights in the front yard and adorned with a 6-foot Christmas wreath with a gigantic red bow. The new room looked nice: big windows, lovely roof-line. But it was nearly as big as the original house, and made it now easily the biggest house on the block. Steve was appalled. Even Jennifer was taken aback.

Her dad greeted them at the door. "Hey, Merry Christmas!" He gave his daughter a big hug, and shook Steve's hand warmly.

"Merry Christmas, Bill," Steve said.

Jim and Karen were there already. Out of the corner of

his eye, Steve could see Angela off by herself in the kitchen, headphones on, listening to music. She looked up briefly, then away as the family members continued to greet one another and coats were hung up and Christmas packages set aside. The formalities didn't take long. Then Bill was all over Steve.

"Well," said the older gentleman, "what do you think?" He was looking at Steve with a mischievous twinkle in his eye.

"Well, Bill, I think we're happy to be here, and I'm glad to see all of you."

"No, not that! What do you think about my guest room? Isn't it great!"

"Well, I..."

"Come on in here and have a look. The plumber did the rough in today."

"The plumber?!"

"Sure! Haven't you been checking the website? I decided to put in a full bath. We need one on this level. It'll be great! Come have a look at how we're blowing your inheritance!" Bill put his arm around Steve, leading him toward the construction zone. To Steve, it felt like the Twilight Zone. As they headed off together, Steve was aware of his wife shooting him one last look of warning.

Part II

Angela was nervous. She had been working all afternoon to transform her living space into a banquet hall of sorts. Now she was hustling around to get things ready: setting the table, lighting candles. Grandma Gladys was right: The ham was easy. And everything else was falling into place. Angela had insisted on getting the dinner together all on her own, as a way of saying thank you and the only Christmas present she could manage. Grandpa and Grandma volunteered to take care of the baby for the afternoon. As Angela worked, she thought over the events of the last year.

It was in February that she had discovered that she was pregnant. Marriage to Gavin was never a serious option. Their whole relationship had been based on things that were pretty much the opposite of stable family life. He was gone in a heartbeat. Angela's parents had gone through the roof. They saw just one way out of the situation; they tried to pressure Angela into having an abortion. But as Angela worked with the counselors about that, she realized that that just wasn't something she could do. She thought long and hard about adoption, too. But she really wanted to raise this baby.

When her parents threw her out, Angela had no place to go. Grandma Gladys and Grandpa Bill had taken her in as the first resident of Grandpa's new guest room, and the family pretty much blew apart at first. Angela's parents more or less disowned her. But with her grandparents' support, Angela kept on with her computer classes and was able to do really well. She had graduated in the spring. Her parents wouldn't come.

"Give them time," Grandpa had said, "they'll come around."

But Jim and Karen were still so angry that they had even stayed away when Jamie was born. That was six weeks ago now, though it seemed like six years.

Let's see…how many places to set? Grandpa and Grandma, Aunt Jennifer and Uncle Steve, me with the baby… should she bother to set a place for her parents? Grandpa invited them and they didn't say they wouldn't come; you'd think they'd want finally to see their grandson. Sure, they were against her having the baby. But things were going to be all right. Angela had a good job starting the first of the year, and an apartment to move into just a few blocks away. Grandpa and Grandma would keep helping with the baby while Angela got her feet on the ground. It was going to be hard, but it would work.

Angela was startled from her thoughts by the ringing of the doorbell. Early! Somebody's an hour early! This is not what I was counting on! Quickly, she looked out the window to see if she recognized a car, but there was none in sight. "Grandpa!" she called. "Grandpa, there's somebody at the door." But, hearing no response, she moved to open it herself.

It was a man she didn't know, an older man. He was quite a sight: gaunt, gray hair unkempt, two or three days beard, eyeglasses askew, a far away look in his eyes. And, strangest of all, he was wearing pajamas and slippers. Angela wasn't frightened, exactly, but she certainly was unsettled by the man's appearance. "Grandpa!" she called again. "Grandpa, please come! There's a strange man at the door!"

Suddenly, Grandpa was right there, his voice strong and calm. "My dear," he said, "this is no stranger. This is my dear friend, Wallace. Come in, Wallace, come in. Come in out of the cold."

For a man in such a state of confusion, Grandpa seemed to be treating him with respect, almost deference. "Angela," Grandpa said, "Wallace and I worked together for nearly 40 years. He is always welcome in my home."

Little by little, Grandpa related the story. After his wife's death, Wallace had become increasingly confused. His one son lived in Alaska. So Wallace was living in his own apartment with a daycare arrangement that worked sometimes and sometimes just didn't. From what they could tell, today he had simply wandered off and amazingly found his way to

Bill's house.

"He's confused," Gladys said later. "He doesn't know where he is."

"Well, for now," Bill replied, "he's home."

Part III

"You silly old fool," Gladys scolded. "You had no business getting out there in this weather. If you are too sick to go with me to Bible study, you are too sick to be out shoveling sidewalks."

"Innocent as charged," Bill replied. "I've been sitting right here in my chair, looking out this lovely picture window and admiring the view. Jamie came over and shoveled the walk before school. Made quick work of it, too. He couldn't wait to try out the snow shovel I gave him for his birthday. Ten years old and that kid really made the flakes fly. Obviously he takes after his grandpa!"

Gladys laughed. "Just wait until the shine wears off that shovel and Grandpa's lazy streak comes to the surface. We'll be back to doing our own walk in no time."

"I'm not so sure about that," Bill replied thoughtfully. "That kid's a worker. And he really has a special feeling about this place. He knows he got his start here. Right here."

"It's kind of funny how things worked out this year," Gladys responded. "I was trying to remember the last time we didn't have somebody living with us at Christmas. For a stretch of years, there it was just one thing after another."

They were quiet together for a moment. "How was Bible study?" Bill asked his wife.

"Oh," she replied, "it was a little strange. I can't quite get used to doing themes instead of books. Today we were talking about hospitality: Abraham entertaining those three strangers who turn out to be angels, the 23rd Psalm and, 'thou preparest a table before me in the presence of mine enemies.' Then we talked about Christmas and there being no room at the inn, and then something I'd never noticed before from Hebrews."

She fumbled around with her notebook. "Here it is: 'Do not neglect to show hospitality to strangers, for by doing that some have entertained angels without knowing it.' The minister mentioned that 'angel' just means 'messenger,' and that made everybody think a bit. We talked about welcoming God, and Florence Weatherby asked whether we had ever felt God come into our lives, whether we had ever entertained angels. Then Phyllis Milton said she had a great recipe for angel food cake, and the class just laughed. But what do you think? Have we… entertained angels, I mean?"

She couldn't help but notice that his eye glistened as he answered her. "Yes, we have," he said. "I'm sure of it."

2003

I think it was Mark Twain who told the story of a young man who went away to college, came home, and was astounded at how much his parents had learned while he was away. One of the motifs for those of us planning worship at Christmas is the need for "exiles," particularly returning college students, to experience everything as they remember it. With so much that is new in their lives, home becomes a symbol of stability, and church plays a role in that as something traditional from year to year: same hymns, familiar lessons and anthems. But faith needs to grow up along with our understanding. So sometimes we try to help returning students see church in a new light, too—to understand that faith speaks to all the changes in their lives. It's a tough balance to strike. At the time this was written, our older son was a junior in college and the younger one a senior in high school.

"The More Things Change"

Part I

Nathan had a sinking feeling in the pit of his stomach. The truth of it was that he was ready to be done with this semester. Not that it hadn't gone well, especially for his first extended time away from home. He had made a lot of new friends at college. And although his classes were a lot of work, his early fears that he wouldn't be able to cut it had melted away as he got into the swing of things. On the whole, he really liked college and appreciated the huge difference from high school. But enough was enough.

What prompted his sense of "no mas" was a little impromptu quiz by Mr. Stevens, his teacher for the year-long Bible as Literature class Nathan had enrolled in with such high hopes. Mr. Stevens was tremendously popular: a remarkably funny man who seemed to have read nearly everything and who brought the Bible alive in startling and amazing ways. Nobody who had heard it could ever forget the lecture he offered each year on the first day of class. It dealt with the first chapter of the Bible, Genesis 1. Stevens went through the story of creation and drew on the board a picture of what was being described: first there was water everywhere, in three dimensions; then there was a dome that created an air space within the great expanse of water—a clear dome, which is why the sky is blue, supposedly, because there's water up there; then the waters down below are parted and land appears under the dome. It went on like that for a while, with students staring in amazement at this drawing that looked nothing like the universe we know, yet a clear and accurate depiction of what Genesis says. Usually by the time Stevens got around to hanging the lights up in the dome, the sun and the moon and the stars, kids were laughing out loud. The upperclassmen had told Nathan about that first lecture, and it didn't disappoint.

The semester had gone on like that. Most of the stories they picked apart Nathan had never even heard; admittedly, he wasn't much of a Bible reader. A lot of the kids loved it, poking holes in stuff they had never quite learned in Sunday school, making fun of the pre-scientific world view of the Bible. But some of the kids got pretty upset. Usually by mid-semester break, all the fundamentalists who had signed up with the idea of fighting with Stevens were gone. In Nathan's class, Jennifer seemed the last holdout. Everywhere he saw her on campus she always seemed cheerful—almost annoyingly cheerful—with a big smile on her face.

But lately when it came to Mr. Stevens' class, Jennifer's smile was missing in action.

The final exam had been over the whole semester's work on the Hebrew Bible, and Nathan had done pretty well. Or so he thought. He wrote his term paper on the "poetry of the exile," something that would have meant nothing at all to him just a few months before: writings in the psalms and some of the prophets that depicted what it felt like to be completely uprooted from everything familiar and carted off to a strange place with new customs and foreign rituals. Nathan had really gotten into it because, to his way of thinking, it was a lot like going away to college.

Today, the final meeting before Christmas break, was supposed to be a teaser about next semester, which would cover the Christian Scriptures—what Nathan was used to calling the New Testament. But the teaser turned out to be a quiz over the Christmas story, and it wasn't going at all well. Nathan had learned from a semester of sometimes painful experience that when something in Mr. Stevens' class seemed easy and obvious, it was probably wrong.

"Forget what you think you know" was the motto he drummed into his students. Usually that wasn't so hard for Nathan. But he thought he knew something about Christmas. This quiz was easy. Something was terribly wrong.

"OK," Mr. Stevens called out. "Grade your own. We won't count this." Nathan's ears nearly popped with the change in pressure as the whole room emitted a sigh of relief.

"Number 1: Where was Jesus born? Anybody... anybody... Buehler?" Laughter broke the tension and a girl in the front called out tentatively, "Bethlehem?" "OK, Bethlehem: how many of you think Jesus was born in Bethlehem? Let's see your hands! Well, you're right. Maybe thought I'd get the easy one out of the way first."

"Number 2: How many kings are mentioned in the Christmas story of the Gospel of Mark?" Nathan was feeling pretty confident on this one, relying on his background in Christmas carols. He decided to chance it: "Three? We three kings of Orient are?"

As soon as it was out of his mouth he wished he could reel it back in, but he sensed right away that he was now on the other end of the line and had swallowed it hook, line and sinker. "Three? How many think Mark mentions three kings in the Christmas story?" To Nathan's relief, about half the class raised their hands. "Well, you're wrong on that one. There is no Christmas story in Mark. Neither is there one in the Gospel of John. Luke and Matthew are the only places we find Christmas stories, and they are quite different from one another, which leads us to...question number 3: How many kings are mentioned in the Christmas story of Luke's Gospel?"

Nathan was into this far enough now that he might as well go the rest of the way: "Three? We three kings of Orient are?" Mr. Stevens looked at him and smiled. "All right, Nathan! If at first you don't succeed…How many think that Luke mentions three kings in the Christmas story?" There were fewer takers this time, just a smattering of hands. "You are wise to be cautious!" Mr. Stevens cackled. "Luke doesn't mention any kings in his Christmas story…which leads us to question number 4: How many kings does Matthew mention in his Christmas story, Nathan?"

"Well, Mr. Stevens, since we've ruled out Mark, John and Luke, I'd have to say that Matthew mentions three kings: 'We Three Kings of Orient Are!'" Everybody laughed. But they weren't getting off that easily: "All right, class! For 50 points and three weeks of vacation from my harassment, how many agree that Matthew mentions three kings?" Nearly the whole room raised their hands, except for Jennifer, who sat with her arms folded and a sullen expression on her face. She was surprised to hear her name, "Well, Jennifer, it seems that you are the only remaining skeptic. Do you think Matthew mentions three kings?"

She wasn't having fun. "Probably not."

"Well, you're right. Matthew mentions visitors from the East, but never mentions their number, and they are not kings. They are magi, astrologers, wise men, something like Babylonian priests, from the Middle East, but certainly not from the Orient. We three kings of Orient are? Wrong, wrong and wrong. But Matthew does mention one king in his story. It's King Herod, and he is decidedly bad news."

At that moment the bell rang, and students quickly gathered their books to begin to leave. "For those of you who are continuing with the course," Mr. Stevens called out above the shuffling and rustling, "you will be well-served to read the Gospel of Mark over winter break. It's short. You can get through it in an hour and a half or so. And it has no Christmas story. Happy holidays!"

As they were leaving, Nathan looked over at Jennifer. He couldn't help himself, and he asked, "So...was it good for you, too?"

She looked at him strangely at first, pondering the vaguely sexual reference. Then she laughed out loud. "Sometimes I don't know what I'm doing in here," she said as they walked toward the door. "I think that Mr. Stevens is a good man and all, and a wonderful scholar. But I think sometimes that he just takes delight in trying to take faith away from people. I wonder what he thinks he's doing."

"Yeah, I see what you mean," Nathan replied. "I don't think it hits me as hard as it hits you. I mean, I went to church some when I was a kid, but we were never all that wrapped up in it or anything. But I think it all means something to me. Now it's like I've got a Mickey Mouse watch that just sort of works, so he takes it apart and leaves the parts scattered all around the room, and I don't have a clue how to put things back together. I don't know. I'm just looking forward to being home for Christmas, where things will be the same and we won't have to think about stuff so much."

Part II

Nathan sat alone in his room and reflected. This was not what he had been expecting at all. He thought back to the fall and how eager he had been for school to start, how happy he was to be getting away from home, how much he looked forward to new things and new experiences. He was ready to be outta here. He would never forget the look on his mother's face as she reached out to hug him goodbye, the terrible sadness in the way she had clung to him. His father, too, had been an absolute spectacle, a first-class mess, the two of them just devastated that their baby boy, Nathan, was all grown up and gone away to college.

But now that he was home for Christmas, they were behaving as though he didn't live there anymore. They had painted his room while he was away. They gave away the bedroom furniture he had had since he was a boy. And here he was sitting on one of those new space age mattresses from the late night infomercials in a room he could hardly recognize. His parents were supposed to be paralyzed with grief that he was gone; where did all of their energy come from?

And Christmas was all different. The tree wasn't in the living room anymore; they put it in the family room, because they said they'd see it more in there. The outside lights that had been on the hedge out front every year he could remember, that he and his Dad always put out on the Sunday after Thanksgiving, weren't there this year. "Not worth the bother," his Dad had said. Dinner was going to be different on Christmas Day. "We thought we wouldn't make all that mess with a turkey again at Christmas," his mother told him. "We just finished cleaning up from Thanksgiving. Too bad you couldn't come home then, but something simple and quiet will be better for Christmas, since it's just the three

Just the three of us. That was the worst of it. His brother, Matt, for the first time in their lives, was not coming home for Christmas. He was going to spend the holiday with his girlfriend's family skiing in Colorado. That news had hit Nathan particularly hard. He had exclaimed to his Dad, "Not coming home? How could he not come home for Christmas?"

His dad just smiled and said, "Ah, you can't fight hormones, son. You can always tell people who are in love, but you can't tell them much."

Some Christmas.

Nathan was trying not to feel sorry for himself, and not to take it out on everybody else, but it was a losing battle. When his parents had suggested that they open presents on Christmas Eve instead of Christmas morning the way they always did it, he didn't even have the heart to protest. Sure, go ahead, ruin my Christmas, ruin my life, if you don't care, why should I, was what he wanted to say. But all he said was, "OK."

He didn't feel like Christmas. He didn't even feel as though he was at home. He didn't know what to do. His parents seemed so happy in their new life. His brother was far away. Absentmindedly, he began to empty his backpack and put some things on the new table in "his" room. There was a CD of Christmas music. Ordinarily he just loved to listen to familiar carols, but not today, not here. He set it aside. And then, almost surprisingly, there was the notebook from his Bible as Literature class. As he turned to put it on the table, his term paper slid out onto the floor. He picked it up and began to page through it.

The poetry of exile: "By the rivers of Babylon—there we sat down and wept when we remembered Zion. On the willows there we hung up our harps. For there our captors asked us for songs, and our tormentors asked for mirth, saying, 'Sing us one of the songs of Zion!'" Sing us a Christmas carol, Nathan! Let's have some of that good old music from home! But the poet so far from home went on to say what now was in Nathan's heart: "How could we sing the Lord's song in a foreign land?"

"Well," he thought, "at least I'm not the first person who ever felt as though home had been pulled out from under him." He began to reread the paper, seeking at least the comfort of being reminded of a job well done. A B+ from Stevens was nothing to sneeze at.

The big thing he had learned was that a lot of the poetry of exile was filled with hope. But the hope didn't come from the exiles' circumstances. It came from their trust in God. And all of their yearning for home, their yearning for Jerusalem, was a symbol of their hope for God's deliverance. "Strengthen the weak hands, and make firm the feeble knees. Say to those who are of a fearful heart, 'Be strong, do not fear! Here is your God.'" Do not fear. Here is your God. Where had he heard that sort of thing before?

Part III

How many times had he heard that lesson from Luke? Every year he could remember. Nathan could just about recite it from memory. But as he sat with his parents in the candlelight service, it was as though he had never really heard it before. It's poetry to exiles, he thought to himself. What the angel says, it's as though it is spoken to lost and weary travelers who just can't seem to find their way home again.

"Do not be afraid," says the angel. It seems as though messages from God always start out that way. "I am bringing you good news of great joy for all the people..." for all the people. "... to you is born this day in the city of David a Savior, who is Christ the Lord." Hey, all you exiles, listen up! You don't have to be afraid any more.

Do not be afraid of feeling lost. Here is the way. Do not be afraid of the darkness. Here is the light. Do not be afraid if you cannot find your way home; here is the fulfillment of home's yearning come to you.

Suddenly, the whole story seemed different to him. This baby who was born in the darkness, so far away from his own home, was the most beautiful poem to exiles that God has ever shared.

Nathan was quiet as they left the service, but strangely

uplifted as they went about the rest of their Christmas Eve. They did open their presents, and it was fun. There were fewer gifts than he remembered, partly because there were just the three of them. But they took their time with it, and they laughed a lot. It was different from the frenzy of Christmas mornings when he was a kid, the two boys tearing into packages like a couple of tornadoes. But the difference was good. When they were all finished, he didn't feel empty, as he had thought he would. He felt OK.

His dad let out a yawn and announced, "Well, it's way past my bedtime. I am going to sleep."

"Me, too," said his mother. "Are you staying up, honey?"

"I'll be up in a little bit," Nathan told his mother. "I'm just going to sit here a while and look at the tree. Thanks for a terrific day. I'll see you in the morning."

"You bet," said his mother as she gave him a kiss. "Coffee cake for breakfast tomorrow. We always have coffee cake for breakfast on Christmas morning."

Nathan just smiled.

2004

This is the story I wrote in the car as son Paul and I drove back to Des Moines following his first semester at the University of North Dakota. The place is very specific: the parsonage in which I lived in Branford, Connecticut, complete with the little detached one car garage out back. Careful conversations with extended family are not unknown to us. And Mr. Brookman is inspired by a man who did some landscaping for us, complete with the New England accent. His circumstances, however, are completely fictitious. Unexplained pregnancies always have a place in Christmas stories.

"Out Back"

Part I

"Mr. Scrooge," the voice on the radio began, "at this festive season of the year, it is more than usually desirable that we should make some slight provision for the poor and destitute, who suffer greatly at the present time. Many thousands are in want of common necessaries; hundreds of thousands are in want of common comforts, sir...a few of us are endeavoring to raise a fund to buy the Poor some meat and drink, and means of warmth. We choose this time, because it is a time, of all others, when Want is keenly felt, and Abundance rejoices. What shall I put you down for?"

"Nothing," replied Gary, finishing the conversation himself as he reached over to turn off the radio.

"You wish to be anonymous?"

"I wish to be left alone!"

And alone is where Gary was, in his little shop in the converted garage out back. When they had first moved into the tiny, Cape Cod-style home nearly 20 years ago, Ruth, his wife, had commented that the small, single car garage was hardly big enough to house both the car and Gary's workshop. A succession of cars had been left out in the cold ever since.

It was more than a workshop. It was a sanctuary of sorts, a place where he could be alone with his thoughts. The opportunity to work with his hands was a welcome counterpoint to the head-work of teaching at the college in their small town; and over the years, he had gotten to be pretty adept at woodworking. Gradually their home had filled up with his projects, early bookcases and coffee tables gradually giving way to Mission-style furniture for the living room, a hutch to display their china and a table and chairs for the dining room. With finals just over and Christmas only 10 days away, this was prime workshop time. Ruth knew that he would have a project underway, but she didn't know what it was.

This year, it was a new bed, queen size. The mattress and box spring had already been delivered and were leaning against a wall and concealed beneath a blanket. He was down to the handwork on the headboard and footboard, the side rails having been completed. Gary was now enmeshed in the familiar internal struggle that accompanied the end of every project…trying not to grow impatient. He had trained himself over the years to slow down as the end approached, to savor the last few tasks and to give them extra care. It meant that he spent a lot of time in his shop, but as the frenzy of Christmas approached, he liked it that way.

Ruth had learned to go her own way as far as their entertaining was concerned. She made the arrangements, and he was on a "need to know" basis. "As long as I don't have to get dressed up for company," he told her, "you can invite anybody you want."

The obligatory visit from the family of Ruth's brother, Ray, was scheduled in shifts this Christmas. That's because when Ray's whole family came over for Thanksgiving, the combination proved overly combustible. Ray was a pretty serious type, and an ardent Republican who had not yet recovered from the heady experience of what he considered vindication from the electorate. At Thanksgiving, the elation was still new; and Ray was hard-pressed to forego reminding everybody that he had been on the winning side. "Mandate" was a word Ruth and Gary had heard enough of for awhile.

But even that was all right on its own. It was when Ray got together with his son, Steve, now a student at the college, that the pyrotechnics really ensued.

Steve was something else. Ray sometimes joked that Steve must have been left on their doorstep by gypsies. He was the ultimate free spirit, whose antics seemed tailor-made to get under his father's serious skin. Steve sported a scraggly beard and long hair, which he generally stuffed up under one of a variety of hats he liked to wear. He had a raging sense of humor and an iconoclastic streak that had made his first semester something akin to the arrival of an asteroid.

In just a few short months, he had organized a new cheering section that went to the football games, and with perfect diction rose as one and said things like, "Harass them, harass them, compel them to relinquish the elliptical spheroid." He sponsored the "Who Cares Film Festival," featuring *A Thousand Clowns, Ferris Buehler's Day Off, The Big Lebowski* and *Dating Do's and Don'ts,* a social etiquette film from the 1940's. His newest project was called F-FASOPE the Future Flight Attendants' School of Prepositional Emphasis, in which participants would do dramatic readings of a range of literature, placing emphasis only on the prepositions, as in, "IN the case OF an emergency, lighting will appear IN the aisles leading you TO the nearest exit." The winning reader did a stirring rendition of the Gettysburg Address: "Fourscore and seven years ago, our fathers brought forth UPON this continent a new nation, conceived IN liberty and dedicated TO the preposition." Steve was quick-witted, and on a mission to stamp out anything that seemed to him to be too serious: in short, the kind of college student everybody enjoys...as a part of somebody else's family.

But when he was around his dad, Steve's good-natured fun managed to take on a biting edge, which had taken a big bite out of everybody's Thanksgiving. The official Lighting of the Fuse took place when Steve announced his conviction that the greatest filmmaker of the current generation is Michael Moore. At that point, Ruth resolved to have Steve and Ray over one at a time.

Steve had finished his exams yesterday, so last night was supposed to be Steve's night to come over. But with predictable unpredictability, he didn't show. Tonight they were expecting Ray, who was driving in to stay overnight with Ruth and Gary before driving back home to Chicago with Steve in the morning. Well, so much for planning.

"Hey, Distinguished Professor Uncle Gary! How's it going? What's Iowa's answer to Norm Abram up to this Christmas? Maybe a toilet seat out of teak or an SUV out of cedar?"

"Oh, hi, Steve. How did your first finals week go?"

"Not so bad in a sleep-deprived sort of way. I really crashed after my econ final yesterday. Probably would have been a good idea to open the book before the last week, huh? I don't know what my father sees in that stuff. Think I passed, though."

"Well, first semester finals are a rite of passage for a lot of kids. Maybe next semester you'll get started a bit earlier?"

"Yeah…or maybe not!"

"Fair enough. Looking forward to going home?"

"It'll be good to see some of my friends from high school. But honestly, I don't know how I'm going to manage being cooped up in a car with my dad for six hours or so. That's a lot of lecture time."

"Well, Steve, I have faith in your capacity for self-defense. Just try not to make him too mad, OK?"

"Sure thing. And you'll be having the same conversation with him, I trust?"

"Well, probably not. But I do expect to be seeing him. Maybe I can put in a good word for you. He's supposed to stay with us tonight."

"Gary," Ruth's voice cackled over the intercom. "Come on in. Ray's here."

Steve smiled a wry smile. "Oops! I think I was supposed to be here yesterday."

Part II

In fairness to everybody, it should be duly noted that things didn't go south right away. Efforts were made—indeed they were—to keep things civil. Gary tried to steer the early conversation toward sports—usually a pretty safe common ground for fathers and sons. And this offering came at some sacrifice to Gary and Ruth, who couldn't care less about the Chicago Bears. But when it comes to the Bears, who generally have one outstanding player at a time—meaning one per generation—before long, there just isn't that much to say.

What was it that set them off? Probably it had been the war. When Steve revealed that he had written a history paper on nonviolent resistance to the draft during the Vietnam War era, and that he was working with the chaplain's office to get ready for the new draft that he was sure would begin any day… things sort of went downhill from there. And suddenly the room was suffocating, filled with heat and no light.

At times like this, Ruth's side of the family became her sole responsibility. "I'll be out back," Gary announced. And everybody knew that things had gotten out of hand again.

It was a crisp and clear night, with the stars so vibrant that it seemed you could reach out and touch them. And even the few steps from the back door to the garage were enough to help Gary feel as though he were entering a different world.

Things were winding down inside, but he could still hear the voices behind him. So he switched on the radio, which was playing a rerun from some old Lessons and Carols service from England. He had heard them for so many years that he had all but memorized the prayers. This was an old one, because the vicar's voice from years ago had always reminded him of Jacob Marley. "Beloved in Christ," he began, "be it our care and delight this Christmas Eve…" and the voice droned on and on, so comforting in its familiarity.

"It's strange," Gary thought to himself. "These prayers are so beautiful. Imagine all the people around the world who are hearing this, or who heard it once whenever this first was broadcast. They have done this in times of war and peace… at Christmases when people have lost loved ones or started families. People have grown old listening to this stuff. It's something they can count on."

His attention returned to the Jacob Marley voice, "And let us at this time remember in his name the poor and the helpless, the cold, the hungry and the oppressed; the sick in body and in mind and them that mourn; the lonely and the unloved; the aged and the little children; and all who know not the loving kindness of God." Off his thoughts went again, wandering the Christmas paths of his mind, so that he did not notice he was not alone in the workshop any longer.

The man cleared his throat behind Gary. "'Scuse me, sir," he began. "Name's Brookman. I was walking down the street and noticed your light. Didn't mean to disturb ya."

Gary looked him over and quickly determined, however

we manage to make these determinations, that he was nobody to fear. The man was short of stature and slight of build, but with strong hands that looked as though they were accustomed to hard work. Beneath the battered Red Sox cap, his wiry hair was gray and receding. Gary guessed him at something like 40. But when people work hard outside, it can be tough to tell.

"Well, Mr. Brookman," Gary said gently, "what can I do for you?"

"Well, sir, me and the missus has been on the bus all day. This is as far as our ticket would take us. We're here to make the best of things, whatever that might turn out to be. There was nothing open near the bus station. Is there a place where we might be able to get something to eat?"

"Well," said Gary thoughtfully, "there's nothing like that open downtown. We have convenience stores and the like, but they're all out by the interstate, and that's about three miles from here."

"Eh-yah. I seen that when we come into town. So we need to walk back out there?"

"Well, I don't know about that. Where's your wife?"

"She be right here." A slight woman stepped into the light of the doorway. Gary could see immediately that she had had rough treatment. The man noticed Gary noticing.

"Don't get the wrong idea, mister. I ain't the one did this to her. And he ain't never going to hurt her again, if I have anything to say about it."

"Would your wife like to sit down?" Gary motioned toward the sole chair in the workshop.

"I'd be grateful, mister," she said. And as she moved toward the chair, Gary could see that she was pregnant.

"We're not exactly married yet, sir," the man continued. "But we're planning on it soon as we can. And I'm gonna help her look after the baby. We just need some way to get a start."

"Well," said Gary, "let's start by going into the house. There's plenty to eat in there, and I imagine the folks inside can use something new to talk about."

Part III

Christmas morning was calm and quiet as Ruth and Gary opened presents. They had been with families with children on Christmas, and that was fun—the frenzy, the delight, the eagerness to play with all the new acquisitions. But they had their own rituals. Sleeping in after the exertion of going to the late service the night before. Opening first the new fancy coffee that Ruth gave to Gary every year. Savoring the aroma and heating up the homemade coffee cake. Looking at the silly things they put in each other's stockings. It was nice.

Usually the last element of the ritual involved a trip out back.

As the last of the coffee was nearly gone, Gary found his voice. "Ruth, I have a confession to make."

"Well, I hear that confession is good for the soul."

He smiled faintly. "I hope so. There's nothing out back this year."

Ruth's voice registered more surprise than disappointment. "Really? Well, what in the world did you spend the entire fall doing out there?"

"Oh, I worked on a project, all right. And I was thrilled with the way it came out. It was something we've been talking about for years...a new bed. I was really pleased with the handwork I did on it...a real labor of love, all right."

"Well what happened to it?"

"I gave it to the Brookmans."

"You did?"

"I did."

"You hadn't done enough for them? You got him that maintenance job at the college, and got Dr. Smedford to do their prenatal work pro bono until the insurance kicks in. You brought them to church and introduced them around as though they were our own relatives. You helped them find an apartment. And now you've given them a bed?"

"Well, Ruth, that apartment looked pretty empty to me. I don't know. Maybe I got carried away."

"Oh… I think you did just fine."

"So you're really OK with this?"

"Some total strangers show up like something washed up by the tide and you give them the best thing you have? I'm more than OK with that. I think that's about the best Christmas present ever." They sat quietly for a moment, then Ruth looked up with a twinkle in her eye. "Besides, that leaves you with something to work on, doesn't it?"

Gary smiled. "You always did see right through me, dear. Merry Christmas."

2005

In September 2005, Priscilla and I went to Cincinnati to help my best friend die. This was the first Christmas following his death, and grief was in my thoughts and on my heart. He had three children. Even the barrenness of grief is not without its gifts and graces.

"You Never Know"

Part I

Maybe it wasn't such a good idea to take a whole afternoon off from work just for this, but Steve thought it was important. For months, he had been dreading getting out the stuff for Christmas, but he knew the day had to come, and this was it. He was ready for a good cry. Some folks are avoiders. But not Steve.

Opening the boxes of decorations was like diving into a time capsule. Maybe it was the faintly musty smell, but years of memories came flooding in on him. To his surprise, what he remembered most vividly was the blur of putting things away last January. It was just before Catherine was to begin her last round of tests. He shuddered now to think about it.

Whenever Catherine had put away the decorations, everything was just so: neatly packed up, fragile items on the top, carefully padded and protected. But last year she had not been up to the task, and Steve had had to do it, more madness than method. Everything was all in there together: stockings and tree ornaments and loose figures from the many crèche scenes they had collected over the years; along with the children's books they had gotten out and displayed ever since the kids had been young. This would need some sorting through.

And there it was: the Christmas scrapbook that they had added to every year, memory upon memory. He had wondered where this had gotten to—at the time of the funeral they had been looking around for pictures to display and couldn't find these. If I get started with this now, he thought, I'll never get through it. I'll just set it aside for the moment. As he turned to set the scrapbook on a nearby chair, something loose fell out. It was a program from the Lessons and Carols Service they had gone to in England four years ago—Catherine's dream of a lifetime to go to King's College, Cambridge on Christmas Eve. "Thank goodness we did that," he thought. "Thank goodness we didn't put everything off."

In dropping to the floor the program had fallen open to the bidding prayers at the beginning of the service. Steve had always been touched by the part that says,

And because this above all things would rejoice [the heart of Christ], let us at this time remember in his name the poor and the helpless, the cold, the hungry and the oppressed; the sick in body and in mind and them that mourn; the lonely and the unloved; the aged and the little children; and all who know not the loving-kindness of God.

Catherine had always loved this service, and Steve had grown to love it, too. He got over the stuffiness of it and fell in love with its elegance. It had just never occurred to him that one day he would be one of the people they prayed for: "them that mourn."

He had probably never even noticed what comes next: "Lastly let us remember before God all those who rejoice with us, but upon another shore and in a greater light." "Upon another shore and in a greater light": at that, he just let the tears come.

Then he got angry. "God, I hate this," he said out loud. "I hate it that these stupid little things set me off and I am so helpless." He was angry with himself for being so exposed, so vulnerable even after all these months. "It's emotional incontinence," he thought to himself. "I never know what's going to get me started." He reached for a tissue as he thought, "It's a good thing I took the afternoon off." He just didn't want the kids to see him like this anymore.

His sister, Julie, said that he and the kids should just come out there for Christmas. But there was something just plain wrong with spending Christmas in Arizona if you didn't live there. One can play only so much golf.

On the other hand, his friend, Hank, had really leaned on him to do everything exactly the same as they always did, for the sake of the kids: "Stick to your traditions" was Hank's wisdom. "The kids need that anchor." But Steve thought that was pretty crazy, too. You can't just go on as though everything's the same when clearly it isn't. And you can't just run away and hide on a golf course.

No, this was the right way for them to do it. The only thing for him to do was to keep going. He picked up the scrapbook to reinsert the order of worship and flipped open to a page with a picture of a Christmas pageant. There were the kids, probably about 15 years ago: Ken was a wise man,

David was a shepherd, and little Kate (what was she, maybe four?) was an angel. That was the year the boys taught her the Lord's Prayer, and told her to say, "Lead a snot into temptation." Steve got a good laugh out of that. Maybe he'd make it through this, after all. Over the phone, he had told the kids to be prepared to improvise.

Part II

He should have checked the status of the flight on his computer before he left the house. They had been delayed 90 minutes. "I should have known," Steve thought to himself. "It was too good to be true that they're all coming in on the same plane from Chicago. Something had to go wrong." Briefly he considered his options. If he went back home, by the time he got there it would almost be time to turn around and come back. He'd just wait here at the airport. He could use a little down time.

The weeks leading up to Christmas had flown by. He got the Christmas cards out. And he managed to get a tree up, even though the ornaments weren't on it yet; they could do that together. Christmas dinner was the one thing he had decided to simplify drastically: some nice steaks would take the place of the big turkey dinner they usually had.

Improvise. Steve decided to sit in the airport lounge and have a beer while he waited. He winced briefly at the airport prices, wished the bartender a Merry Christmas, and found himself a table alone near the window. The sun was beginning to set over the tarmac. In the distance, he could see the lights of an approaching plane. He took a sip and sighed deeply.

He glanced over to the area outside security where people were gathered to welcome loved ones. Two young children were bouncing up and down and shrieking with anticipation and delight as a new wave of people came down the stairs and the escalator. I know just how you feel, kids, he thought. Inside this aging façade, I'm doing the same thing! He checked his watch. He still had over an hour to wait.

On the TV was one of those pseudo-news programs, an investigative report about the "real" story of Christmas. He tuned in and out as the reporter interviewed a number of scholars regarding the biblical stories of Jesus' birth.

They were talking about Bethlehem. "There was no room at the inn," Steve chuckled as he remembered traveling in the car with Catherine. She had confided to him one time that whenever they passed a motel with a No vacancy sign, she would feel a little bit of regret, almost a sense of rejection. It wasn't that she wanted to stay there, but that she knew that even if she wanted to, she couldn't. The range of her options, in the grand scheme of the universe, had been limited somehow. She had seemed a bit surprised to learn that not only did he not share this sense of constraint, he found it very funny. He would tease her whenever they passed a world class dump; one of those places from the 1950's where all the rooms are separate shacks. "Look, Honey! I think they've got room. I know it's only 10:30 in the morning, but maybe we should stop there!" No room at the inn—better improvise. Make it home wherever you are.

He thought again of his kids and how proud he was of them. Ken and David were working near Boston and had left there on the same flight. Kate was in school in Chicago, where the three of them were meeting to fly in together. Since their mother's illness and death, they talked on the phone more than they ever had before. It was a great comfort to Steve that they could support each other.

The darkness deepened, and the stars were beginning to show. Gradually, the scene outside disappeared, to be replaced by Steve's reflection in the glass. He found the effect unnerving, the new view uninteresting. He turned again to the television.

The reporter was describing how shepherds watching their flocks at night were frightened nearly to death by a sudden incursion of angels. One of the scholars, a slight man with white hair and an Irish accent, was saying that whenever people hear from God, the very first part of the message is always the same: "Fear not! When people are in the presence of God, they always have enough sense to be afraid."

There are a lot of things that will put the fear of God in you, Steve thought. He reflected back to the scene in the hospital months ago when Catherine had died peacefully, quietly—a moment of such holiness and such peace. It was a God moment—not frightening, really—but filled with awe.

But what do you do when God drops out of the sky on you with glad tidings of great joy? There you are, minding your own business, and God just shows up. You never know, do you? Here we are, just minding our own business....

Isn't it annoying, Steve thought, the way they pace the commercials on these programs. They start out about 20 minutes apart, and then when they think they've got you hooked the commercials get closer and closer together. Everything peppered with urgency: Last minute! Sale! Hurry! But the one that really made him laugh was the one inviting everybody to hurry up and return the stuff they got for Christmas...and then buy even more.

Steve looked at his watch one more time. Another 20 minutes. He found himself getting more and more excited. The program was back on with a bit about King Herod. The wise men came looking for a new king, and so they went to the palace in the capital city. But when they got to Jerusalem, all they found was Herod, a power-crazed Roman puppet who was unstable even on the best day of his life. Herod had no qualms about killing his own family when he thought they were trying to wrest power from him.

Whoa, boys! Steve thought. Steer clear of that guy! Get out of Jerusalem! Plan B stands for Bethlehem. And isn't that just how it goes? We plan things out, figure just how they're going to go, and then it all goes another way. We do all the things we're supposed to do to get ready for Christmas, and then Christmas comes—or doesn't—when and where it's good and ready. Start out in a cozy home in Nazareth and end up on a pile of hay in O little town of Bethlehem; set out for the ease of a Holiday Inn and find yourself shacked up with the beasts; look for a king in a palace and find a peasant child in some hick backwater; spend years nurturing cherished family traditions and find yourself in this hollow time with an empty place at the table. He was lost deep in thought.

"Wait a minute! Did they just announce the Chicago flight?"

Part III

It really wasn't his idea, and Steve couldn't remember who suggested it first. It was the steaks that had gotten them thinking about something different…somehow it was just too much for the kids to handle: Christmas in July sounds like fun, but a July barbecue at Christmas is just too weird. One of them—one of the boys, perhaps—had mentioned how much Catherine used to talk about the people who were alone at Christmastime, how she had rung bells for the Salvation Army and bought and wrapped gifts for poor families through the church. And then somebody said that maybe they could help serve Christmas dinner at the shelter.

A phone call was all it took, and they spent the middle of their day, from about 11 until about 3, helping to serve turkey and dressing and mashed potatoes and cranberry sauce and green beans with onion rings (whoever started that, anyway?) to a bunch of people who were in no particular hurry to get Christmas dinner over with. Surprisingly, there were a lot of people there to help serve. And so they ended up with each of them focusing on a table of eight or 10, keeping the serving dishes filled, freshening up everybody's coffee and just sitting down to chat. No hurry. Just conversation.

One of the guests took a shine to Kate and offered her a

gift. "Here, Missy," he said. "I don't have much use for this, but maybe you'll enjoy it." It was one of those disposable cameras, and it proved to be just the thing. Kate went around taking pictures of her brothers, her dad and some of their newfound friends on Christmas. These would prove to be some unusual additions to the Christmas scrapbook.

All in all, it certainly gave the day a different rhythm from what they were used to: the long-remembered frenzy of flying paper and ribbon and the sugar buzz from cookies and candy and the odd, sleep-deprived, hung-over feeling everybody usually had all day. This was sure different from that. But it wasn't a difference that was just something being taken away from them. It felt like something new—a difference that was oddly like a gift.

More than anything, it felt like something Catherine would have loved. Whose strange idea of a Christmas was this? Nobody's. If they had sat down to try to think of something, the idea might never have come. Here they were, just doing the best they could, and it came to them.

These things are funny. You never know.

2006

Inevitably, I envision this story as taking place in a small college town like Grinnell, but the house is our house in Omaha—I associate late night feedings with a rocking chair in that house. The role of the College Chaplain grandfather is played by Dennis Haas, who was the chaplain at Grinnell during my student years. I'm not sure who Martin is, really… but I have known a lot of curmudgeonly iconoclasts over the years. Most of us are protecting tender hearts when you come right down to it. The music Martin hears as he's feeding the baby is "Candlelight Carol," written by John Rutter and done beautifully by our Chancel Choir. "Jesus" is a form of the name "Joshua."

"Candlelight Story"

Part I

"You are not going to ruin this for everybody," Claire said, sternly pointing at him for emphasis as she spoke.

"There's that finger," Martin said, hoping to kid his way out of a tight spot. "Whenever you point the finger, I know I'm in trouble. But I have done nothing wrong."

"Oh yes, you have," Claire rejoined. "Every time anybody mentions Stephanie's Christmas pageant you smirk and roll your eyes. But I don't care what you think about Christmas, and I don't care what you think about pageants. This event is not about historical veracity or about religious doctrine. This is your granddaughter's Christmas pageant, she is going to be an angel, she is very excited and you are not going to ruin it for everybody with your tedious and self-important philosophical analysis. Have I made myself clear?"

"I suppose that's clear enough," Martin said quietly. "But you could be a bit more pleasant about it. I mean, after all, the finger..."

"Would you like to see a different finger? No? Well then

promise me that you'll behave yourself. Julie and Jacob will be there with the newborn. Dennis and Ann will be there…you can hang out with Dennis. Ann's father will be there…four generations. This is what we call a family event, and you will not ruin it for everyone."

"Oh, come on, Claire," Martin said, beginning to get a bit defensive. "I know you and I found each other a bit later in life and that I am new to this business of being a stepfather and a grandfather. But I don't think that my presence in and of itself will be a problem to anybody. And as to my religious convictions, or lack of the same, I fail to see why it is necessary for all of us simply to shut off our brains just because Christmas or Easter or whatever rolls around."

"Here it comes," Claire said, "I can feel you starting to warm up, and we are not going there this evening."

Martin ignored the Do NOT ENTER sign written in large letters and smashed right through the barricade. "I do not think it so inappropriate that we raise questions about this completely improbable story," he began. "The business with the shepherds and the angels and the wise men and the star is crazy enough. But how about a woman who is nine months pregnant riding a donkey from Nazareth to Bethlehem? You have to be completely ignorant both of obstetrics and of geography to find that remotely plausible. And the thought of foreigners bestowing priceless gifts on a poor peasant family is ridiculous. And the suggestion that King Herod would slaughter babies in Bethlehem and that there would be no corroborating independent historical record of such an act is beyond absurd. The story, at best, is metaphorical, and should be acknowledged as such. Why do we teach these things to children and encourage them to accept such stories as though they were history? This is no more historical than *The Wizard of Oz* or *The Cat in the Hat.* The only people who benefit from what we're doing are purveyors of biblical literalism and therapists who later on will have to help these children unlearn the drivel they have absorbed in their youth!"

Claire had one more try left in her. "Listen, professor. It's Christmastime, and you are not going to ruin this evening for the whole family by telling your granddaughter Stephanie that what she is doing amounts to silly superstition. Adults can fend for themselves. If you want to debate Christmas, debate it with Dennis for the 10,000th time—how the college chaplain and the village atheist ended up best friends still escapes me, but since his son is married to my daughter and these are his grandchildren, too, he will be there and you can amuse yourself with him, but you will keep your cynical asides to yourself or you will stay home. Understand?"

"Claire, you are being really unfair about this. I think I

have as much right as anyone else to express an opinion, and I should think that the grandchildren would benefit from knowing that not everybody feels the same way about these ridiculous stories. Don't you think it would be healthy to have a discussion of the story after the pageant so that Stephanie can begin to realize…"

"No, I don't, and I'm sorry I brought it up. I love you, but tonight you're staying home. I will see you later."

She ignored the startled look on his face, kissed him on the lips and was gone before he could recover. But Martin had to admit that he felt more relief than injury.

Part II

How did this happen? Martin looked over at the infant in the car seat, for the moment at least asleep on the table, and he tried to reconstruct the evening. He had fallen asleep in the chair—that much was clear enough. So he hadn't even been aware of how late it had gotten. Then suddenly Claire had burst into the family room carrying the newborn, Joshua, and breathless with the story. Dennis's father-in-law—Ann's father—had collapsed at the church. They called 9-1-1 and he was rushed to the hospital, with family trailing along behind. Martin's stepdaughter Julie and her husband, Jacob, had both the kids with them—Stephanie (still dressed as an angel) and the baby. Stephanie refused to leave her mother, but they thought it best to get the baby out of the hospital. Since Martin and Claire lived closest, Claire took the baby home to leave him with Martin and then went back to the hospital to wait with Julie and the rest. Yes, that was it.

Whew! In any event, here was the baby.

Martin tried to clear his head and remember the instructions. Little Joshua would need to be fed during the night. He would wake up crying. Change the diaper first—he had done that a couple of times, though he was hardly practiced at it. Then warm up the bottle, feed and burp. It seemed clear enough. But with a little luck, the kiddo might just make it through the night or until reinforcements arrived. Martin resolved just to leave him where he was, on the dining room table, all bundled up and in the car seat. Why go looking for trouble?

The ringing of the phone roused him from his thoughts. It seemed so loud that it fairly shattered the stillness. It was his friend and the other grandfather, Chaplain Dennis. "Hey there, Grandpa," he began, "How are you doing?"

"Oh, I think we're all right," Martin whispered a bit tentatively. "Joshua is still asleep for the moment." But even as Martin said this he could tell that the baby was beginning to stir. "How are things on your end?"

"They think it's his heart," Dennis said. "Ann wants to stay here—she's really close to her dad—and Julie wants to stay, too, and Stephanie refuses to leave Julie, so Claire is intent on staying to help. That leaves me as sort of the odd one out. I wondered if you'd like to do a grandfatherly double-team on Joshua."

"That would be wonderful," replied Martin, who could tell that it would be just a matter of moments before the next infant eruption. "You're a good deal more experienced at these things than I am, and I would appreciate the help."

"Be there in about half an hour," Dennis said.

But it was soon evident that reinforcements would arrive too late. Baby Joshua was at the end of his patience, squirming and screwing up his face as he began to cry. Martin fumbled with the car seat and began to work his way through the layers of clothing that swaddled the baby. As each layer gave way, the distinctive odor grew more intense, and Martin didn't have to wonder what was inside this Christmas package.

All in all, that part went pretty smoothly. And so did the bottle. In fact, it was almost magical. Martin could not believe the peace and the trust he felt from this little child as he fed contentedly and gazed up into Martin's face. "I'm an impostor," Martin wanted to tell him. "I don't really know what

I'm doing. It's a mistake to trust me." But the baby seemed content, wrapping his tiny hand around Martin's little finger.

The room was almost dark, except for some candles that Claire had lit hours ago. Their flickering light lent a warmth to the scene. "I bet he could go to sleep," Martin thought to himself. "What do babies need to fall asleep? Music! He reached out for the remote, pointed it at the CD player and hoped something appropriate was in it. Christmas music… of course. Claire loved Christmas music.

The gentle sound of a choir filled the room, singing words Martin hadn't heard before. "How do you capture the wind on the water? How do you count all the stars in the sky?" There was the ancient imagery of creation, Martin thought, the breath of God blowing across the waters of chaos and the placing of stars in the firmament. The song continued: "How can you measure the love of a mother, or how can you write down a baby's first cry?" How, indeed, Martin thought as he gazed into his grandson's eyes. Human love is as infinite as the heavens, and each life as wonderful and inexplicable as the universe itself.

The song enveloped them almost like a spring rain, making everything new and fresh and clean: "Candlelight, angel light, firelight and star glow…." Yes, that's what we do when we don't know what else to do. We light candles and we bathe in the sense of mystery. When the philosophical abstraction fails, we turn to poetry. When the infinite eludes us, we find it in the intimate. When we lose count of the stars, we find the same sense of limitless wonder in the trusting eyes of a baby.

"Candlelight, angel light, firelight and star glow shine on his cradle till breaking of dawn, *Gloria, Gloria, in excelsis Deo*! Angels are singing, the Christ child is born." That's what the story is trying to say, isn't it? The infinite is in the intimate. Whatever we think of as God is found at the very heart of the wonder of life itself. God is right here, in the eyes of this child.

Martin and his grandson sighed at the same moment.

Part III

How long were they there? Surely it was longer than half an hour...but time became irrelevant. When he finally arrived, Dennis was surprised at the scene he found. With the familiarity of an old friend he let himself in through the side door, and came quietly into the family room where Martin was gently rocking the sleeping child as Christmas music continued to fill the room.

Dennis sat down and just smiled.

At last he said, "Well, professor, what is my silence worth to you?"

Martin didn't speak, but the puzzled expression on his face invited Dennis to elaborate. "Well, here is the distinguished skeptic rocking an infant by candlelight and listening to John Rutter Christmas music. Honestly, Martin, if I didn't know better, I might think you were going soft on us."

Martin just smiled and shrugged his shoulders.

"Anyway," Dennis resumed quietly, "I'm sorry it took me so long. Ann's father is coming around, and it looks as though he's going to be all right. The doctor came by just as I was about to leave. I said I'd be by in half an hour; it's been more like an hour and a half. Sorry."

Again, Martin just shrugged as if to say, "No problem."

"What's the matter, old friend? Nothing to say for once in your life?"

Martin looked up. "Doesn't one of your Christian mystics—a Quaker or some such thing—say something like, 'Never say anything that won't improve on silence?'"

Dennis just smiled, and the two old friends sat together quietly.

2007

There are a number of real elements in this story, beginning with the dog Pixie, who stars as herself. And the family nicknames are all genuine, too, if nicknames can be genuine. This story is set in our Des Moines house. My wife, Priscilla, collects nativity scenes, and they're all over the house at Christmas. The school building in Carol's dream is McClellan School, my grade school in Pittsburgh. But that dream sequence in the second part of the story was something new for me. It felt like taking a chance, but I was fascinated by it when I wrote it. I still am.

"The Pageant"

Part I

Carol sighed deeply as she sat for what seemed like the first time all day, taking just a moment or two to catch her breath before moving on to the million and one things she had to do. She smiled as she wondered again, "How did I get into all of this?" It had been shaping up as a fairly sane Christmas—perhaps the first one since Craig had died four years ago. Then she found out that she would be on call for the holiday… bummer. Then she shot off her big mouth, first to her parents: "If you want to see Holly and Bill and me this Christmas, you're going to have to come here. I won't be able to get away." She was sure they wouldn't leave the warmth of the sunny southwest, but she was wrong.

They were driving from Arizona with Pixie the micro dog, a paranoid little bundle of mixed-breed hyperactivity who, every time you looked at her sideways, trembled and peed on the floor. Pixie was a love-project that Frank and Gloria were trying to mold into being her very best little canine self. Carol smiled. They had a long way to go, but that kind of love was something they were good at.

Carol delighted in her parents, really—no problem there.

And they would certainly help to keep Holly and Bill occupied when Carol had to work. But the possibility of a low key Christmas had gone out the window right there. Her father, Frank, was a positive-thinking doer, full of energy and activity, the life of the party. And Gloria was a helper, always tidying up and baking cookies and the like. This will be good, Carol thought. This will be good. She sighed again.

But nephew Tony was the real surprise. In October, Carol and Holly and Bill had gone to Colorado to attend Tony's—Carol still wasn't exactly sure what to call it: Commitment Ceremony? Holy Union? Marriage?—to Tony's longtime partner, Gabe. It was a deeply meaningful and joyous occasion for all those who went. Tony and Gabe clearly brought out the best in each other, and people relished seeing them together and witnessing their vows. But Carol's older brother, Tom, had refused to come to share this moment in his son's life. That was so sad for everybody, Carol thought. But it was saddest of all for Tom.

Carol laughed out loud as she thought about her son, Bill, and the nicknames he had for all the members of the family. There was Uncle Patriarch and Aunt Vulture, the last of the grandparent generation on Craig's side. And Carol's brother, Tom, and his wife, Ann, he called Uncle Redneck and Aunt Inane. Families!

At the ceremony, Carol had said to Tony and Gabe, "Listen, you two! My brother will come around. He just needs a little bit more time. I'll keep working on him. But if you would like to come to our house for Christmas, we'd love to have you." It seemed like a good idea at the time. Now Tony and Gabe were on their way from Colorado and bringing two more dogs: Spike, a little toy Pomeranian who specialized in noisily attacking his favorite squeaky toy, and Balthazar, Gabe's Rottweiler, who specialized in being calmly formidable. Encroaching canine chaos: the more, the merrier!

Which was probably why, on impulse, Carol had called her brother, Tom, and left a message on his answering machine: "Hey, brother," she had said. "I don't want to run your life for you, but I wanted you to hear this from me before you heard it any place else. Tony and Gabe are coming here for Christmas. Now before you say or do anything you are likely to regret, please just think about this: We'd love to have you with us. Won't you please come and share Christmas with your son? Mom and Dad will be here. We'd like to all be together, and we can't do that without you." She heard nothing for three weeks. Then her brother sent an e-mail: "Arriving for Christmas 12/23." That was all it said. Whew!

No doubt about it: This was going to be interesting. We all go through a process, Carol thought. She remembered a conversation with Holly the previous summer, as they were driving back from the service in Colorado. Holly had gone into sullen mode, sulking and pouting and sighing until Carol finally said, "All right, young lady! I can't read your mind. What's the matter? Don't you approve of Tony and Gabe?"

Holly looked out the window as she said, "That's not it, exactly."

"Well, what is it, exactly?"

"Oh, I don't know. It's Gabe. I mean, you know he's so… so…"

"So gay?"

Holly looked shocked. "No! That's not it."

"What, then? So African-American? So tall? So Presbyterian—I think he's a Presbyterian?"

"Mother!"

"Well, what is it, then?"

"Oh, he's just so…so flashy, so fancy. Everything he does is like really stylish, and Tony has always been just…simple. Tony is all about corduroy and blue jeans and hiking boots and earth tones. I love the way they are with each other, but this clash of styles really bothers me."

Carol chuckled. "Well, you know, relationships are all about negotiation. They may have differences of style, all right, but I don't see many differences of substance. Do you?"

"No, not really, I guess. And Gabe is so funny and kind. I just hope they'll be OK. Tony seems happy, and he deserves to be happy, don't you think?"

"Holly," her mother replied, "I think everybody deserves to be happy. It's just that it seems as though some of us can't stand it for very long."

Well, for better and for worse, they were all coming. Carol was roused from her thoughts by the flash of headlights on the ceiling. Bill had just pulled into the driveway, home from college. Here we go, she thought, as she reviewed her mental list: leaves in the table, chairs up from the basement, rearrange the living room, clean towels and linens all around, newspapers on the floor by the door for Pixie…help had arrived. She rose and moved toward the door to greet her son.

Four hours later, Carol was seated once again. Holly was in bed. Bill had gone out with friends. She savored what she assumed would be some last few minutes of peace. She looked over at the table where she kept her collection of nativity scenes—or a few of them, at least. They were all over the house. One of them, a *nacimiento* from Mexico, was elaborate and ornate, with hand-painted, glittering gold figures with beautiful halos seeming to radiate from Mary, Joseph and the baby Jesus. Another, also from Mexico, was very simple, made from unpainted clay in earthen colors. Another was from Africa, with tall, gaunt, stately, dark-skinned figures posed in the same familiar story. Attached to the wall behind the table was yet another nativity scene, from Bolivia, this one encased in a box with doors that stood open to reveal a three-dimensional scene in which the angels seemed to swarm overhead—an elaborate, colorful and almost chaotic image of celebration. To the side, from Eastern Europe, was an Easter egg that opened to reveal the Christmas scene. And a recent acquisition was a scene with figures from the story *The Best Christmas Pageant Ever*: 1940s kids in T-shirts, overalls, dungarees and sneakers depicting the biblical tale. Carol sighed again and closed her eyes for a moment, listening to the Christmas music playing gently in the other room.

Part II

It began with the sensation of a tiny dog licking her face. And then, in the distance, a sound of music, rhythmic and insistent: bump, ba-ba-bump, ba-ba-bump, ba-ba-ba-ba-ba-ba; bump, ba-ba-bump, ba-ba-bump, ba-ba-ba-ba-ba-ba. It was a kind of primitive march, and gradually, it grew louder and louder. The dog, wearing a collar that had the name "Spike" embroidered in it, kept licking Carol's face until at last she picked him up and set him on the ground, where he danced in tiny circles. And it was ground: grass, a field of some sort, like an athletic field.

Everything was enshrouded in fog at first, but eventually Carol could see a light off in the distance. There was a building there, a brick school building, and it made a sort of an L where two wings came together. That was the spot the light was coming from, and Carol began to walk toward it.

Two figures, a man and a woman, were huddled over a box. The man looked up; it was her father, Frank. He was beaming his life-of-the-party smile, and he began gesturing broadly to Carol, calling her over, pointing to the box and smiling, then gesturing with both hands as if to say, "Come on! Come on! It's a party! Come on!" Pixie the micro dog pranced around and around the box, now and again jumping up and looking in, then going back to prancing. Now the woman looked up, and it was her mother, Gloria. She had something in her hand. It was a feather duster. She began to sing.

Suddenly, back behind her, Carol heard the sharp sound of a whistle. It made her think of a drum major. She turned to look, and there was Gabe. He looked magnificent in a gleaming golden cape, and he had a radiant halo. He turned toward Carol and blew the whistle once again, and a brass ensemble began to play "Hark the Herald Angels Sing." Gabe looked up toward the sky, lifted the edges of his cape and very slowly at first he began to spin. Ever so gradually, he twirled faster and faster. And then he tilted to the side and continued to spin so that the cape became a glorious disc of color. Round and round he went until all that could be seen was the radiant swirl which ascended into the night sky and gradually moved toward the building, closer and closer to where Frank and Gloria were gazing into the box, gesturing and beaming.

Carol moved to follow Gabe as he soared and swirled, drawn, as was Carol, toward the scene before her. There was singing now, a huge chorus with the brass singing "Hark the Herald Angels Sing," and people appeared from every direction in long lines streaming toward the building. They came in every size and color, wearing the dress of every imaginable nationality, walking silently, majestically, joyfully in a colorful procession. Carol walked, too. She didn't turn to look at the people around her, but she was aware of them all, a vast multitude converging on the same place, but somehow not crowding together or displacing one another. The closer they came together, the more room there was for each one. They all came closer and closer, drawn toward the disc that was now swirling above the couple and the box.

One by one, yet all at the same moment, they approached, as her father kept gesturing in welcome, smiling and laughing and pointing. Carol drew near and gazed into the box.

What she saw there made her heart swell with delight. How could you describe it? It was a sort of mirror. And as she gazed into the mirror, she saw an image of herself—but not just as she appeared at that moment, but in a single instant of time she was seeing herself as she had been throughout her life and as she would be into the future. In this mirror, she could see the totality of who she was. And she knew that everyone who approached was having exactly the same experience, all in the same moment, seeing themselves—and everyone else—in the fullness of time all in a single instant of eternity. It was all there, and she had never felt so known, so connected, so loved. No wonder her father was laughing. Carol laughed, too—with joy. It was so wonderful! She had the overwhelming sensation of having come home, being at peace, wanting and needing nothing more than to be there.

And she found herself kneeling. Everybody was kneeling. Spike lay down beside her. And there, sitting regally near the box, was Balthazar, Tony's Rottweiler, keeping watch. And that must mean...Yes, there was Tony, kneeling in his jeans and boots, looking as though he had just come in from the fields. And next to him were his parents, Tom and Ann. Of course they were.

Carol glanced at Holly and at Bill. And there was Craig, her husband who had died. Where else would he be? There was no place else for anybody to be.

Suddenly Carol was aware of the sensation of a bright light overhead. And moments later a sound, like a door closing. She heard approaching footsteps, but she didn't want to look, didn't want to move. And then Bill's voice: "Mom? It's 2 o'clock in the morning. What are you doing at the dining room table? Why don't you go to bed?"

Part III

She savored these moments before everybody else was awake, especially today. It almost made having to go to work worthwhile. Even the dogs, exhausted from chasing each other around the night before, barely stirred as she went through her routine: juice and yogurt, toast and coffee. She didn't want to disturb anybody by bringing in the paper. They could get it later; on Christmas morning, it would all be ads, anyway. Sleep in heavenly peace.

How different with the house so full! She and Holly were used to rattling around in the place. Now Frank and Gloria were upstairs in Carol's bed, Tony and Gabe in the basement, and Tom and Ann on the sofa bed in the living room.

They had really filled up a pew in church. And maybe it was just her, but it seemed to Carol that the old story had never seemed so new. She'd be off at 2 o'clock, and everybody had agreed to wait until she got home to open presents. The way they'd gotten into the eggnog, some of them might not be up until noon. Tom had brought along some old family videos of Tony as a boy, and some of the old family reunions when Craig was still alive. And they had laughed. Thank God, they had laughed!

2008

Apart from a few of the details, this story is pure fabrication. But it had its origins in conversations with people who were going away for Christmas, traveling "over the river and through the woods," and who lamented being gone from their own church at Christmas.

"Holy Night"

Part I

Blessed peace at last… relatively speaking, at least. It had taken a frantic flurry of activity, but they were finally in the car and on the way to Katherine's mother's house for Christmas. It was only a four-hour drive; but the interval offered welcome respite from the frenzy. Why exactly had they decided that the family room needed new carpet right at Christmas? And why had the dryer chosen precisely this time to make that odd moaning noise when it started and stopped? And why had their lovelorn dog sitter chosen the day before Christmas Eve to make up with her boyfriend and change her plans for the holiday? Everything seemed to need doing at once. The bird feeder for Grandma had arrived broken. The packages were almost wrapped when they ran out of Scotch tape, so Greg finished them up with duct tape. They had been scurrying and scrambling to get on the road. But now at last they were launched. Brady in the backseat was lost in his iPod, and Greg and Katherine had some moments to breathe.

As it worked out, their timing had a real upside to it—nothing they planned, mind you, but perhaps only because they didn't think of it. With their late getaway, they would not arrive until after 7 o'clock, which meant that they would not have to go to church with Katherine's mother and the rest of the family. Thank you, Jesus! That was a major relief.

It was a nice enough little country church, and the people certainly tried to make things festive and special. But their very part-time, mostly retired pastor, Archibald McCracken, really got under Greg's skin, and Greg had difficulty disguising his disdain. It wasn't that Greg was a Scrooge or hated

Christmas. Quite the opposite. But he thought that the kindly old pastor was so innocuous and inept that he seemed to make a mockery of the solemnity and importance of the holiday—or any holiday, for that matter. And the funeral he had done for Katherine's dad…not only did he use the wrong name at one point, but the eulogy deteriorated into McCracken's reminiscences about being a boy during World War II. It seemed there was no substantive occasion he could not trivialize.

"Just once," Greg had said the year before, "I'd like to hear even the faintest suggestion at Christmas that the baby Jesus grew up and actually did something. I'd like to hear that he got in trouble because he believed in helping common people, that he died because of what he stood for and believed in, and that those who follow him should be committed to making the world a better place. But what we get is sentimental platitudes, an hour of fumbling around and 'Silent Night' on a piano that hasn't been tuned in decades. It doesn't have to be great, but it isn't even terrible. It's the bland leading the bland."

Katherine, bless her heart, knew better than to overreact to Greg's outbursts. She let him blow himself out and then simply said, "But the point is really just everybody being together. It means a lot to my mother when we can all go to church on Christmas Eve. And there's good in everything and everyone. You just have to stop being so critical and look for it."

And that was certainly true enough. Sometimes Pastor McCracken, or McCreakin' as they occasionally called him, supplied some unintended comic relief, like the time he fell asleep during the anthem, or the time he stood up to read the lesson and called for the offering instead, setting off a wild scramble among ushers who had slipped off to have a cup of coffee. Greg wanted to cut the old guy some slack and always felt guilty for being so critical. But comic relief seemed thin gruel at Christmas.

Fortunately, their son, Brady, had been oblivious to all of this a year ago. But it wasn't likely that the controversy would slip by him again. Katherine was not eager for a repeat of last year. So they had had a talk about church, and she had repeated her mantra once again, "You have to let it be special. You have to feel the magic. There is good in everything and everyone. Just listen for the good."

Brady was crazy for Christmas. He started with his Christmas countdown calendar on the day after Thanksgiving. He had on his Christmas socks and his Christmas sweatshirt and his Christmas hat. Last night, Brady had found Greg where he was wrapping presents, and he triumphantly held up a pair of underwear. "These are the ones," he said. "These are the ones I'm wearing on Christmas." He was crazy for Christmas.

Greg glanced at his watch. "Looks as though we'll make it just about 7:15. The traffic has been really good. How did your mother take it when you told her we'd be too late to go to church?"

"She didn't seem too upset. She just said, 'Don't you worry about that. Just drive carefully and we'll see you when you arrive. We have a surprise.' I have no idea. Maybe Uncle Teddy and Aunt Roberta are coming over or something. I hope he doesn't bring that flea-bitten old Santa outfit. No telling what's been living in that beard."

"Well, whatever the surprise is," Greg replied, "we'll just go with the flow. After the past couple of days, whatever it is will be a relief." And he settled into the drive, lost in thought and letting himself slowly unwind.

Greg was right. They arrived right at 7:15. Katherine's mother came tottering out to meet them in the driveway. After hugs of greeting she said breathlessly, "Hurry on in. Dinner's on the table. We'll just have time to eat and then we can still make it to church. They changed the time this year to 8 o'clock. Surprise!"

Katherine looked at Greg and the look said it all. "Listen for the good."

Part II

For better or for worse, they made it all right. They got to church just before 8 o'clock; and, of course, for the only time all year, the little sanctuary was packed. Greg and Katherine and Brady followed Katherine's mother in...and discovered that Katherine's brother and sister-in-law had saved them seats...in the very first row.

The prelude was already underway: a 12-year-old girl was playing the violin, accompanied by piano; which, Greg noted immediately, was even more out of tune than ever. But that was OK. It meant that the piano and the violin both found some of those amazing in-between notes. The selection was "Up on the Housetop." Even in small towns, Greg noted, they aren't teaching religious music in the schools much any more.

"Listen for the good," he reminded himself. "Of course, she's right about this. Don't let yourself get all worked up. There's something good going on here somewhere. Listen for it."

They all sang energetically on "O Come All Ye Faithful," nearly drowning out the piano. That was good. Greg found himself reflecting on the beauty of the language in the hymn. And before he knew it, the familiar scripture reading had begun. It was read by a high school student, who did a very fine job of it. Not needing to worry whether she would make it through, Greg found himself relaxing into the words and being carried off by some of the images as they flowed over him.

"In those days…" [once upon a time] "a decree went out from Emperor Augustus" [who fancied himself divine ruler of the universe] "that all the world should be registered" [right: so that they could be taxed to within an inch of their lives to support Augustus's armies and to pay for all the fancy buildings in Rome]. "Joseph also went from the town of Nazareth in Galilee" [the country-fried center of nowhere] "to Judea, to the city of David called Bethlehem" [a small town just six miles from the capital of Jerusalem—about like Baghdad with its warring factions and occupying foreign troops—right near the heart of the whole mess]. "He went to be registered with Mary, to whom he was engaged and who was expecting a child" [the scandalous couple invited to no one's Christmas party]. "And while they were there, the time came for her to deliver her child" [ready or not, here he comes]. "And she gave birth to her firstborn son" [sounds easy—this must have been written by a man] "and wrapped him in bands of cloth" [too poor for a blanket?] "and laid him in a manger" [welcome to the world, *bambino*, here's the nursery] "because there was no room for them in the inn."

[Cue the shepherds, the resident aliens, low status workers of ancient Judea] "living in the fields" [huddled around the fire, bad hygiene, bad teeth, coarse language, dirt under their fingernails] "keeping watch over their flock by night" [a 24/7 occupation]. "Then an angel of the Lord stood before them" [so it's just one at first, maybe silently stepping into the edge of the light around the campfire] "and the glory of the Lord shone around them, and they were terrified" [of course they were. In those days, light came only from fire, the sun, and God. Who in their right mind wouldn't be afraid?]

"I am bringing you good news of great joy for all the people" [not just the Jews or eventually Christians but all the people] "to you is born this day in the city of David a savior" [careful, buddy: that's a title Augustus likes to reserve to himself; let's not be singing "Hail to the Chief" here] "who is the Messiah" [there you go again with that king stuff] "the Lord" [another word Augustus likes. Here he comes, the helpless baby king, smack dab in the middle of the whole mess.]

She went on to read the rest of it, of course. The angels singing "glory" and disappearing as suddenly as they had come; the shepherds scraping themselves together to go see about this baby who is supposed to be a sign. Mary taking it all in and saying nothing, pondering it in her heart because maybe she alone can see the enormity of it. Right here, right now, right in the middle of it all. God is here, right now.

Greg was roused from his thoughts by an elbow to the ribs. Katherine pointed in front of them where creaky old Archibald McCracken was seated on the steps up to the altar. He had summoned the children to him (all three of them, counting Brady), launched off on a story about birds lost in a storm, wandered to a place of stopping, and sent the children back to their families. Now, poor thing, he was struggling to get up. Greg moved quickly to him. "Here, let me help you."

Part III

The air was crisp and clear as they walked out the front door of the church. The stars were shining brightly, filling up the sky—not like in the city, where street lights obscure the glory of the heavens. Greg paused for a moment on the steps to savor the night.

He felt a tap on the shoulder. "Thank you for the helping hand, young man," said the old pastor. "I'm not as nimble as I used to be, either physically or mentally, I'm afraid. I'd like to turn this place over to somebody younger; but they're not exactly standing in line to serve little churches like this one. Each year, I wonder if this won't be the last Christmas, either for me or for the congregation."

Greg paused for a moment. "If you don't mind my asking, why do you keep doing this? What is it that keeps you going? I can tell it isn't easy for you."

"Oh, it's the story. We need to tell the story over and over, how this night is different from all other nights, how this night helps us see the holy."

"I suppose you're right," Greg reflected. "Except that what makes it different is that it isn't different. The world God comes to in Jesus is the same world we know, where puffed up rulers jerk people around and people jockey for power and the poor are neglected and there is no room at the inn. If this night is holy—and surely it is—then all nights are holy, because this one is as filled with the problems of the world as any other. Only somehow it reminds us that God is at the heart of it all, even the mess. Maybe especially the mess."

McCracken smiled and shook his head. "Whoa! Slow down, Shakespeare! You've been doing some heavy lifting. Whatever in the world got you started on all that?"

"Oh, I don't know," Greg answered. "Just listening for the good. Hearing it all, and listening for the good. Katherine's right: It's here. Merry Christmas!"

"Merry Christmas to all," he replied. "And to all a good night...a holy night."

2009

I never really knew any of my grandparents. Maybe that's why I fell in love with this relationship between a boy and his grandfather. The characters are not based on anyone in particular—at least not consciously. The respect my sons had for my wife's father comes close, but he was decidedly a man of few words, unlike George in this story.

"All the Best"

Part I

"Cherry picking," George said without opening his eyes. He was stretched out in the recliner, newspaper open across his chest. He and Jarrod, his 18-year-old grandson, were alone together, while Jarrod's parents were squeezing out one last workday before Christmas. George and Jarrod had been teasing one another about who was babysitting whom. Jarrod was sprawled on the couch, umbilical earbuds emanating from an iPod, from which something resembling music was blaring into his ears—George could hear it from across the room. In one hand, Jarrod held a remote control for the TV—mercifully muted for the moment, but offering up a new channel every two seconds or so. With the other hand, Jarrod was using his thumb to scroll through text messages on his phone, occasionally pausing to tap out a response unidigitally—with just his thumb. A laptop computer open on the couch nearby was offering up a replay of a college football game. Small wonder Jarrod did not respond to his grandfather.

George tried again, louder: "Cherry picking!"

Still no response. So he opened his eyes, sat up halfway and cranked it up a few decibels: "I said, 'Cherry picking.'"

Slowly, deliberately, Jarrod emerged from his digital fog, his eyes finding focus. He removed one ear bud and emitted a long, exasperated sigh. "Grandpa, I heard you all three times, even when you were talking with your eyes closed."

George sat up, straightened his glasses, leveled his gaze and prepared for some rhetorical sparring with his favorite grandson. Calling on his grumpiest old guy voice, he began, "Humph! How can you hear anything? You're surrounded by gadgets!"

"We've been over this, Grandpa," Jarrod replied with a smile. "We could simplify this whole setup if only some rich, adoring relative would give me an iPhone for Christmas. There's an app that will do all of this, and more. There's even a fish-finder app, Grandpa—take the boredom out of fishing! But, alas, I'm captive-bound and double-ironed in the first decade of the 21st century."

"You don't need another electronic toy! You need to learn how to concentrate! You're multitasking your mind into mush! You have a marvelous genetic legacy—if I do say so myself—that you're squandering on endless distraction!"

"Oh, listen to you!" Jarrod responded. "You multitask all the time. Here you are sleeping, watching TV, reading the paper and provoking me into a conversation simultaneously."

"Touché," George responded with delight, amazed at his grandson's mind and loved this conversational ping pong.

But Jarrod wasn't going to back off while he had his grandfather on the defensive. "So, are you going to explain yourself?"

"Explain what?"

"Explain your outburst. What do you mean by 'cherry picking'?"

"You really did hear that, didn't you?"

"I told you I heard you. So was that just the pitiful, incoherent eruption of an aging mind, or did you have a point?"

"OK. 'Cherry picking' is an expression that refers to a cheap and lazy harvesting of anything—in this case, reality. The modern world is set up to reinforce the idea that life ought to be nothing but the best of the best at every instant. Playlists replace albums so that artists can never make extended statements any more; people formulate instant likes and dislikes and listen only to what they think they like. How do they ever learn anything new? SportsCenter makes us think that existence should be one continuous highlight. Sporting events become huge-screen spectacles to entertain us and sell stuff to us unceasingly, filling every instant and almost making us forget there's actually something going on right in front of our eyes that involves real people—albeit on steroids—and not just pixelated images. Satellite TV gives us 300 channels of garbage to choose from, so commercials don't just lie about products as they used to, they have to entertain us at every moment because the ever-present remote control gives them about four nanoseconds to get our attention before we move on to something else, so everything, even the news—especially the news!—has to be more and more sensational to compete to occupy the four functional brain cells most people have left over. People don't ever have to watch or listen to anything that doesn't conform to their predetermined formulation of the way things are. We cherry pick our way through life, but what we end up with is not the best of the best but some sugar-coated, moronic, artificial, commercialized exercise in collective denial. But real life—real life—is filled with waiting and boredom and inconvenience and uncomfortable truths and experiences that don't necessarily feel good in the moment but that shape character over time."

"Sure thing, Grandpa," replied Jarrod. "Feel better now? I think I've heard this before: You became such a jolly old soul by spending most of your childhood bored out of your mind, and I'm losing out on my chance to grow up to become just like you…right?"

George couldn't help it. He laughed out loud.

"Grandpa, how about if I go back to picking cherries and you go back to counting sheep and I'll wake you up in time for lunch?"

"OK, little Socrates," George replied. "Talk to you later." And then, just as Jarrod reinserted his earbud and turned back to the TV, George added quietly, "You know I love you, don't you?"

Jarrod didn't reply. George wasn't certain whether he heard or not.

It was probably about half an hour later when Jarrod

surfaced again. Then things seemed to happen in a hurry. Jarrod looked over at his grandfather and got an eerie sensation that something was terribly wrong. His face looked crooked and there was fear in his eyes. Jarrod asked him if he was all right, and he seemed to try to answer, but the words came out all garbled. Terrified, Jarrod first called his mother at work and described the situation. "Jarrod," she said, "don't try to do anything with Grandpa. Call 9-1-1 right away. They'll tell you what to do. I'm starting for home. Call me if they take Grandpa to a hospital. Hurry!"

Part II

And then, after all the hurry, there was nothing to do. The emergency personnel wasted no time. Inside of 10 minutes, they were whisking George away to the nearest hospital. He was still confused and unable to talk, and had effective use of only one of his hands. But he kept pointing toward the chair.

Finally Jarrod got it. "Your bag, Grandpa? You want me to bring your bag?"

He nodded ever so slightly and squeezed Jarrod's hand. And then they were gone. Not allowed to ride in the ambulance, Jarrod had waited for his mother. Together they followed to the hospital.

And then…waiting. It seemed to take forever for them to get George out of Emergency and into a room in intensive care. And then…they waited. Visitors were allowed in to see the patients for 10 minutes every hour, so most of the time Jarrod spent in the waiting room. There was one TV there, but it had been taken over by a family with three small children, and they were hooked on the cartoon channel, which was running one Christmas cartoon special after another. *The Grinch…Frosty the Snowman…Rudolph the Red-Nosed Reindeer…*now they were watching *A Charlie Brown Christmas.* A doctor had emerged and taken Jarrod's parents into a family conference room. Jarrod was left alone, sitting on a couch with his head in his hands.

He tuned in and out of the noise going on all around him. He found himself thinking about his grandpa and being really scared. He couldn't clear his mind of the sight of him lying there confused and helpless.

A Charlie Brown Christmas had gotten to the part where the kids put on a Christmas pageant and Linus, in that inimitable, delicate voice, begins to recite the Christmas story from the Bible, from the Gospel According to Luke. Exhausted and alone, Jarrod closed his eyes, and felt the familiar words wash over him.

"... there went out a decree from Caesar Augustus that all the world should be taxed..." What kind of a government is it that thinks it can tax the whole world?

"...with Mary his espoused wife, who was great with child..." Pregnant? And they were only engaged? Jarrod thought about Rachel Miller who had disappeared from school in the middle of last year and shown up in the fall with a baby. A baby! How old is she? Maybe about Mary's age...

"...because there was no room for them in the inn." Jarrod remembered the time the whole family went to South Dakota to see the Black Hills and the motel messed up their reservation and there was no place for them to stay for miles and miles around because of the big motorcycle rally at Sturgis. Such a helpless feeling...and imagine: a woman in labor!

"And there were in that same country shepherds abiding in the field, keeping watch over their flock by night." Talk about a boring job!

"And lo, the angel of the Lord came upon them, and the glory of the Lord shone round about them; and they were sore afraid." A scary angel: Bob Dylan, the 100-year-old angel of the Lord, good news that scares you half to death. And this is how God enters the world? God enters this lost and lonely, boring and terrifying world? God is in the mess of it, the mistakes of it, the reality of it.

"Jarrod?" Lost in thought, he hadn't even heard his parents approach with the doctor. His mother sat next to him on the couch and gave him a big hug. "It's good news," his mother said. "We think Grandpa's going to be all right. The doctors think he's had a TIA. It's a temporary…" She turned to the doctor for help.

"It's a Transient Ischemic Attack. Initially the symptoms are very much like a stroke, but they go away very quickly and the patient recovers completely. He's already regaining his speech and movement, and feeling a lot better."

"He's going to be all right?" Jarrod could hardly believe it.

"We think so, yes. There are a few more tests we need to do. And sometimes a TIA is a sort of warning—we'll need to watch him closely for the possibility of a real stroke. But he's feeling a lot better now. And he wants to see you."

Part III

What a difference. George was sitting up in bed, holding a cup with both hands and drinking through a straw. He looked really tired, but his eyes looked right. He was back. Jarrod took a step toward the bed…and dissolved in tears. His grandfather reached out to him.

"Hey, kiddo," he said. "It's all right. I'm going to be OK.

Take it easy there." But Jarrod just held on for dear life. It was a couple of minutes before he was able to speak.

"Oh, Grandpa," he said. "I was so scared. I thought that maybe the last thing you said to me was 'I love you,' and I'd never get to tell you that I love you, too."

"I know you do, Jarrod. I know you do. We kid each other a lot, but I am so proud of you, and I'll always love you. Always. Now...don't you wonder what's in the bag?"

"What bag?"

"The bag I had you bring along. It's right over there. Don't you wonder what's in it? Bring it over here."

George reached into the bag and pulled out a wrapped Christmas present.

"Here you go, Jarrod. With love from me to you."

Jarrod eyed it suspiciously. "It looks a little big for an iPhone."

"No fooling you," George replied. "It's not an iPhone. It's way better than an iPhone. Open it up."

Jarrod ripped it open in an instant. It was a book with a leather cover...a photo album...filled with pictures from a magical day they had spent together last summer, just the two of them, out on the lake. One of the pictures was familiar: Jarrod and George holding a stringer of fish between them, dinner for the family and a trophy of a great time together.

But the rest of the pictures seemed odd. They were pictures of Jarrod, maybe 20 of them…just sitting. At first he just looked bored: head in his hands, body all slumped over, adolescence in its lowest energy state.

But about halfway through, the pictures seemed to change. Jarrod was still sitting, but he seemed thoughtful, attentive, even enthralled. He studied the pictures for a moment.

"See a difference?" His grandfather asked gently. "Do you see a little before and after? I took every one of these pictures before we caught any fish. What's the difference?"

"Well," Jarrod said slowly, "it was so beautiful out there: the way the light reflected on the water, the sound the loons made, and remember the beaver that swam right by the boat? It was all so gorgeous! That's what I was looking at."

"And how long did it take you to notice that it was so gorgeous?"

"Well, I guess it, uh…it took me a while, didn't it?" His grandfather just waited. "It took me a while of being bored to realize that more was happening than I thought; that there was beauty all around me that I wasn't seeing; that I was just a very small part of something huge and beautiful; that…"

"That what?"

"That maybe it's all the best. That every moment is precious in its way. That when we tune out everything but the highlights, even the highlights lose their meaning after a while." He laughed. "People knock themselves out with presents and food, and what everybody ends up remembering is something silly—like how you rattle the newspaper when you snore or how really little kids would rather play with the wrapping paper than the presents. It's like all of it—life—is holy, somehow. Is that what you had in mind, Grandpa?"

"No, Jarrod. That was way better than what I had in mind. Way better. Come here." He held out his arms to his grandson. "Merry Christmas."

2010

This one felt a bit risky, suggesting that an experience in worship could make a difference that would last, suggesting that people listen to the rustling of their spirits and respond to them, suggesting that a relationship with God is what we hunger for, but that we flee from it when we lose ourselves in the details of church business. The quote about church fights being so nasty because the stakes are so low is from the late Otis Young, former Senior Minister of First-Plymouth UCC in Lincoln, Nebraska. Verla and Dorothy were actual combatants in yet another church, but their battleground was the kitchen, not the parlor...variations on a common theme. The men's group is AMENS.

"Born a Savior"

Part I

"Great! Isn't that just Great!!" As he pushed the off button on his iPhone, it took all Brian's self-control not to heave the thing across the room. "What am I supposed to do now?" he said to the empty room, but he said it loudly enough that his wife, Karen, heard him from the kitchen and responded. "What is it now, dear?"

Brian hesitated. He knew that if he walked into the other room he might get wisdom and understanding, but for the moment, he just wanted validation for his frustration and rage. To talk about it ran the risk of seeing it as less deliciously awful than he was letting himself think it was. Karen was too practical; she would never stop with, "There, there… it must be terribly difficult for you." He decided to chance it anyway.

"Do you believe these people?" he demanded as he strode into the kitchen. "Verla has pulled out." Karen was massaging marinade into a brisket and didn't bother to look up. "Pulled out of what?"

"The parlor carpet. Verla and Dorothy were going to go halves on a new carpet, but they can't agree on a color. Dorothy wants brown and Verla wants green because it will complement the colors in that hideous portrait of her father that her mother painted and gave to the church decades ago. Either one of them can afford to buy a dozen new carpets without batting an eye. Now we're stuck with that threadbare, flea-bitten, moth-infested thing we've got because they can't agree on a color. Unbelievable!"

Karen chuckled. "I believe it. My sister's minister in Lincoln was right."

"Right about what?"

"Churches. He's the guy who said that church fights are so nasty because the stakes are so low."

"Oh, what does he know? He lives in Nebraska, for God's sake! You'd think that just once people could be reasonable and place the greater good ahead of their own petty preferences! What does it matter what color the carpet is in the church parlor? This is crazy! I know what you're thinking: You don't have to say you told me so. I just thought that by going on the Trustees, I could do something to help the church. And I agreed to chair it when nobody else wanted to. I know how to chair a committee...but this is more like a knife fight! I thought we could just sit down and talk this through like adults."

"Uh-huh," Karen said. "And how is that working for you?"

Brian let out an ironic snort. "Not so great at the moment, thank you, Dr. Phil. Not so great."

He walked into the living room and plopped down in the recliner across from the Christmas tree. Christmas music was playing, a choir softly singing carols, but it did nothing to soften Brian's mood.

What is the point of churches, anyway? he thought. The people basically mean well, I suppose. But they're so busy with their little committees and their petty projects. Some of them are so pious that it almost makes you sick: Jesus this, Jesus that, Jesus, Jesus, Jesus. Do you know Jesus Christ as your personal Lord and Savior? But most of them don't talk about Jesus or God at all. The Rev. Stephens is a good soul, I suppose. He's kind enough. But most of the time, it just seems that he wants us to think he's smarter than we are, talking about God as though God were some sort of great puzzle to be solved with church-only jargon: incarnation, absolution, atonement, panentheism and blah, blah, blah, blah. And he's always droning on about who wrote this particular book, what the Greek says and the historical significance of this or that. What's the point? Most of us wouldn't know God if we tripped over God...as though God had anything to do with it at all. Maybe we like it that way. Maybe we do church like this because it's such a good place to hide from God. But, my God, it sure is a lot of work.

Karen delivered him from his delicious but unproductive internal rant. "We're going to need to leave in about 20 minutes."

"Leave?"

"You know about this, for the 7 o'clock service. We have to be there at 6. Kaily is a reader and Brandon is playing his saxophone."

Brian winced.

"Oh, stop that," Karen said, hitting him gently on the shoulder. "You know he's gotten a lot better. We're past the torturing geese stage, and they actually tuned the piano at church this year. He's playing 'Silent Night,' and he's really been practicing a lot."

Brian nodded in resignation. "I know. It'll be nice. It's just that church feels like the last place I want to go right now. I feel like I work there. I feel like I live there."

"Listen, honey," Karen said as she knelt down in front of his chair to look him in the eye. "Do yourself a favor tonight. Just let it happen. Don't think about the dust on the rafters. Don't look around for burned-out bulbs. Don't notice the water stains on the walls. Don't think about the light bill or the heating bill or the carpet or anything else. Just let it happen. Listen to your daughter read and your son play. Sing a few Christmas carols. Let's have a little peace on earth tonight, shall we? Can you try that?"

"I'll try," Brian replied softly. "I really do want to try."

Part II

They were all there. The church was crowded with all the regulars, along with the Christmas and Easter folks who filled in the usually empty spots. Verla and Dorothy were both there early, sitting in their customary pews on opposite sides as if to send the message that neither intended to give an inch, requiring others to climb over them to get to the remaining empty seats. We shall not be moved.

Brian and Karen sat near the front because their children would have to get out to read and to play, so most of the congregation was behind them. Brian was grateful not to have to look at everybody, but he could feel them there. There was more coughing and shuffling and sniffling and whispering than was typical in church.

And Reverend Stephens was different, too. He welcomed everyone warmly as the Advent candles were lit: hope, peace, joy and love. "We need them all," he said. "But especially we need that last one. Love is born tonight." And that struck Brian as the strangest thing he'd ever heard: Love is born. We could use that, all right, he thought. Starting right here and right now, we could use that for sure.

The grade school choir sang a very sweet rendition of "Away in a Manger." No crib for a bed...Jesus, the little Lord. That's an odd image, isn't it, an infant in charge of things? What kind of a world would that be? Brian sighed and tried to do as Karen had suggested—just let it happen.

There were prayers. There was an offering, and Brandon played his saxophone solo on "Silent Night." He did well... sort of splattering the first high note on "all is calm, all is bright." But then he gathered himself and got more secure as he went along, soaring through "sleep in heavenly peace," and coming down with a perfect landing. The full church meant he'd have to play it through twice in order to give them time to let the plates get around, and the second time through was even better. When he had put down the saxophone and slid back into the pew, Brian put his arm around his son. "That was lovely, Brandon," he whispered, "really lovely." He could feel Brandon relax into him and sigh with relief. I wouldn't have missed this for the world, Brian thought.

And then as he looked up, he was almost surprised to see his daughter preparing to read the lesson from Luke. She took a deep breath to remind herself to read loudly and slowly, as her mother had coached her to do. Then she started in: "In those days a decree went out from Emperor Augustus...." She was such a young woman, her voice strong and sure.

But for some reason, Brian flashed back to the first time he had looked into those eyes...and the first time he had fed her at night, just the two of them awake and all the rest of the world sleeping...how time seemed to stand still...and she gazed up at him with an expression of perfect trust. He remembered how his heart had ached; he had never thought it would be possible to love anybody like this. Her tiny fingers gripped his hand as she worked at the bottle, and that moment was all there was.

"For unto you is born this day in the city of David a savior, who is Christ the Lord." The timeless words and his daughter's voice almost brought him back. There it is again: born a savior. "And this will be a sign for you: you will find a child wrapped in bands of cloth and lying in a manger." This tiny, helpless thing, this timeless moment is our window to the deepest truth there is...and I want to give my whole heart in response. Love is born. Love is born.

"O holy child of Bethlehem, descend to us, we pray." Everybody around him was singing now, but Brian sat motionless, tears welling up in his eyes as he heard the words as for the first time: "cast out our sin and enter in, be born in us today." Cast out our...cynicism? Cast out our...hardness of heart? And he found himself praying. "Please, God, could we try this again? Could we just sort of start over, you and I? I feel your love tonight. Can this be a new beginning for us? Help me remember how to love again. Make me be an instrument of your love."

Part III

"How did it go?" Karen asked as she heard Brian come in through the front door. "Was he there?"

"Yes, he was there. I noticed his car parked outside and so I took a chance that he was alone, and he was. I guess he was working on his sermon for Sunday—it's gotta be tough when Christmas is so late in the week—but he didn't act as though I was interrupting him. More like he had all day. He didn't even seem surprised to see me. He said that he had a feeling when I was leaving on Christmas Eve that something was going on with me."

"Well? What happened?"

"I don't think I've ever seen him so relaxed. I tried to tell him what happened to me—as though I could understand it myself—and I thought he'd be surprised or skeptical. But he just said that he thought this was something I should trust and see where it takes me. He asked what happened the next day, whether I found myself praying about it, whether I still have the sense of wanting to make a new beginning with God, almost as though he'd been reading my mind. He asked if I've been wondering whether this is something real or just something I dreamed up, and I wondered how he knew to ask that. He said that this was the kind of experience a lot of people have, but they have trouble finding anybody to share it with so it ends up just sort of fading away. He said it had happened to him...more than once.

"I was surprised, you know, because he comes off as such an intellectual about faith, but he said that for him all the intellectual stuff just gives him permission to feel God, and it's the feeling that's the real place to start.

"Then somehow, we got started talking about the carpet, and I've never seen him laugh so hard. That surprised me... kind of shocked me, really, and I asked him how he could laugh about behavior like that. He said, 'Well, either you laugh or you cry. Besides, we all have a good carpet brawl in us somewhere. You just never know what it's going to take to bring it out.' I suspect he's right about that."

Brian and Karen just sat for a long moment. "So what are you going to do?"

"We talked about that, and he told me to think about it for awhile. But he said I might want to consider taking a leave of absence from the Board. There's a group of men who meet once a week to read books and talk about their faith, he said. And he said that that's a place where they'd appreciate my story, because a lot of them have stories of their own."

"Are you going to do that?"

"I'm not sure. I think maybe I might. All I know is that I think I'm onto something, and I don't want to let it go. And I don't want it to let go of me."

2011

In October 2011, my wife came down with a mysterious condition—neuropathic pain of indeterminate cause—that was terrifying to both of us. Eventually, over many months of living with a great deal of pain, she began to recover. The image of the gift actually came in the form of a Christmas card from Jackie Perry, former Plymouth member, artist and UCC minister, who designed a card with the depiction of a pillar candle. The sensation of the light of a candle touching my heart was an experience I had—not once but several times—sitting quietly in our basement. And, oh yes, the yard display is real. And all those artists are really on my iPod.

"The Gift"

Part I

"Jim?"

"Huh?"

He'd been off in another world. They were sitting at the breakfast table, fortifying themselves for another busy day, with the newspaper spread out all over the place, husband and wife occupying the same space but inhabiting different galaxies. He was looking at the sports page but thinking about all the things he had to do, and how, if everything went just right, he could orchestrate his day to make his meetings at work, get some laundry done at home, wrap some presents while stuff was in the dryer and make some headway on an overdue writing project. It was going to be intense, and he was trying to find the energy.

"Jim! I asked you a question." Those dreaded words! There were so few good options. He could respond with something generic like, "I don't know," or "What do you think?" Or he could pretend that he hadn't heard what Karen said. But the truth was that he hadn't been listening, an entirely different matter and justifiably grounds for a response somewhere on the continuum between reprimand and rage. Occasionally confession—"I'm sorry dear, I was lost in thought"—elicited mercy. This time he settled on a reply that skirted the issue of blame: "Could you try me again, dear?"

"Don't you think it's ridiculous…obscene?"

This wasn't nearly enough help. All he could do was rub his nose in it and take his medicine. "Isn't what obscene?"

Karen gave him one of those "gotcha!" looks. But at the moment her need for self-expression outweighed her annoyance and she plunged ahead. "That thing that the neighbors are doing with their Christmas lights. You know, those people around the corner. They have every inch of their front yard illuminated in some way, and it's all tied into a limited radio broadcast that reaches like a hundred yards and the lights are animated in time to music. So you pull up there and sit in your car and listen to the radio and get a sunburn from this light display that's like Las Vegas on LSD. It's usually some hyper version of Christmas music. But sometimes it will accompany something like 'Silent Night' or 'Away in a Manger,' trying to be beautiful…like a hippo in a tutu. It's obscene."

"Actually, I think Disney did do hippos in tutus in Fantasia; it was kind of cool."

Not about to let him off the hook with laughter, Karen ignored the rhetorical speed bump to proceed. "And sometimes you can hardly get through there for all the cars that are sitting around and watching the flashing lights."

"Well, maybe they're trying to stop and smell the roses?"

"Roses? Hah! You know what they remind me of? The way our dog has to find some foul-smelling spot and rub himself in it! Sitting there in their cars and wallowing in the crassness of Christmas. It's appalling! And it's dangerous. They're right on a curve, and somebody's going to be fiddling with their radio and run right into a gawker sitting there in the dark!"

Jim just smiled and teased her. "I'll have to go check it out."

Finally, she laughed. "Well, you just do that. I'm going to be working late, probably home around 7. Do you want to have dinner together when I get home?"

"Sure. I'll have plenty to keep me busy. Do you want me to pick something up?"

"No, that's OK. I'll do it on the way home."

The doorbell rang. Jim glanced out the window to see the FedEx man already fleeing back to his truck in the pre-dawn light. Jim got up and went to the door to retrieve the package that had been left there.

It was from his sister, Sarah. She was always good for something interesting. Over the years, Sarah had been through her hippie phase and her save-the-world phase and her make-all-the-money-in-the-world phase and her yoga-and-hot-tub phase. But lately, she had settled into what she took to be the best of all that and become a bit more conventional—now that it was no longer conventional—and she was even trying church. Jim had kidded her about it: "I used to be all messed up on drugs, and then I found the Lord. Now I'm all messed up on the Lord." She took his kidding well; but evidently, church really meant something to her.

Karen was scurrying around and trying to get out the door. Jim decided to open the package...just in case there was something alive in there. With Sarah you never could tell.

It was a candle, just a pretty ordinary-looking red pillar candle. And there was a note with it: "May the Light of the World shine in the darkness of your world this Christmas. Love, Sarah."

Karen came flying by for her hit-and-run kiss as she dashed out the door. "What's that? A candle? From Sarah?" She laughed. "Just what we need: another candle."

Part II

What a strange effect this is, Jim thought. He stared at Sarah's flickering candle again. Perhaps it had something to do with the optics of his glasses, but he could see several distinct rays emanating from the candle; not going all around the room, but coming straight toward him. It wasn't the tears that created this effect. Several times, he wiped them away, then he gave up and just let them flow. His eyes welled up and then emptied, and each time, the rays reappeared, beginning from the candle and slowly making their way toward him once again, until there was a bridge of light from the candle to his heart. Strange, and strangely warming.

Jim was sitting in the basement in a recliner, trying to process the events of the past several days. It had all come on so quickly. For a couple of days, Karen was stiff and sore. Then she began to experience shooting pains in her legs. Then she began having difficulty walking. Then she had stayed home from work. And then came the call that she had been taken to the hospital in an ambulance. It was hard for him to admit this to himself, but he was terrified. Seeing her helpless made him feel helpless and made him see how fragile their life together really was. Thank God for the IV. Thank God for the drugs that at last made the pain go away. Thank God for the doctors and nurses. Thank God for the gift of sleep. At last, she had been able to sleep, and he had come home.

He hadn't known what to do, so he'd tried to stay busy. He went down into the basement to get some laundry started. Then he noticed the candle from his sister, over by the table where they were wrapping presents. What had that note said? "May the Light of the World shine into the darkness of your world this Christmas." Somehow now that almost sounded ominous: "the darkness of your world," as though terrible things would happen, or as though he was hiding something, or hiding from something. He wanted to laugh it off. Usually he could laugh. But it wasn't funny.

His iPod was connected to the stereo across the room, all set up with Christmas music to listen to while wrapping presents. "Wrap music," he called it. But that wasn't funny, either. He launched the playlist, imploring a bizarre parade of musical guests to fill up the emptiness of his solitude. And then, on an impulse, he had lit the candle and turned out the overhead lights. I'll just listen to music and wait for the washer to finish, he had thought.

Eugene Ormandy, Dion and the Belmonts, John Rutter, The Blind Boys of Alabama, Elvis, John McCutcheon and the Choirs of King's College all took their turns trying to fill the void in which he was floundering, to hold the darkness at bay in all the nooks and crannies and corners of his heart. And then, all too soon, the music was over, and he was alone with his thoughts...and his tears...and then with the tears alone...and this light from the candle, so strange and unrelenting, so revealing and so welcome.

He remembered something he had read: Listen to your life. See it for the fathomless mystery that it is. In the boredom and pain of it no less than in the excitement and gladness: touch, taste, smell your way to the holy and hidden heart of it, because in the last analysis, all moments are key moments, and life itself is grace. Listen to your life. Life itself is grace. Listen to your life. Life itself is grace. And there is nothing more precious, more holy, more eternal than the gift of this moment.

Part III

Shepherds and magi...stars and angels...emperors and kings...hope for the future...silence and music...and candles. The images washed over Jim as he sat in church and heard the familiar stories once again. One after another, the lessons were read and then interpreted through music. There was light in these stories—he had remembered that; but there was darkness, too. Herod and Augustus and empires ordering people around. No room at the inn, and innocents dying and fearful mystery that is the shadow side of wonder. The light shines…in the darkness.

He felt Karen slide her hand into his. He marveled again that they could be together like this. She wasn't completely well, but she was some better; and they were here together, the busyness of their lives receding into wherever things go when they don't matter anymore. Until she had gotten sick, he hadn't realized that's where all that busyness belongs.

"And the Word became flesh and dwelt among us," someone was reading. God become human, he thought. That's what it all comes down to. And to meet God, we have to be human, too—really human. All of us, not our plans and schemes and intentions and accomplishments and credentials and projects—but just who we are. That's who God came to love, the darkness and the light of us all together. "And from his fullness we have all received, grace upon grace," the reader concluded. Right. And life itself is grace. That's it: Life is grace. That's enough for today.

Jim helped Karen into the car and went around to the other side. Sliding into the driver's seat, he looked over at her and said, "Home, James?" She smiled back at him. "Sure, let's head that way. But let's make a stop. I want to watch those dancing lights."

2012

Mr. Ude was actually a math teacher I had my senior year in high school. He would lose his voice when he put long problems on the board, made a mistake somewhere and got the wrong answer. The issue of the humanness of God seemed a lively one when Matt Mardis-LeCroy and I taught the book *Loving Jesus* in the fall of 2012. Once again, I return to familiar motifs: grandparents and the disarming love of infants.

"Every Heart"

Part I

"So, Jeremy...anything interesting happen in school today?" asked his father, Rick, daring to break the dinnertime silence. Rick had been so busy at work that he was feeling a bit out of touch, and he wasn't at all sure what sort of response he'd get from his 9th grader.

"Well...Mr. Ude lost his voice again today," Jeremy responded cheerfully.

"I suppose I should know the answer to this," his father replied, "but who is Mr. Ude and what do you mean he lost his voice again?"

Jeremy's mother, Julie, intervened: "Mr. Ude is Jeremy's honors English teacher, and he loses his voice when he gets flustered."

"Yeah," Jeremy took over. "It's really weird. His eyes start to water and he starts to swallow a lot and then it's like he can't clear his throat and he makes these weird squeaky noises. Andy Thompson says he's speaking Phlegm-ish," Jeremy laughed. "It's like this other language."

Rick couldn't resist laughing, too. "So why again does he lose his voice?"

"It's like he gets confused or something. Some of the kids like to try to make it happen. But I kind of feel sorry for him. It's not like he can help it or anything."

"And it happened today? Did one of the kids get him going?"

"Not on purpose. We got into this big discussion about anthropomorphism," Jeremy said...and then slyly turned his attention to his plate as though this explained everything.

"Anthro...what?" his dad replied.

"Anthropomorphism. It's attributing human characteristics to something that isn't human, like saying a storm is angry or a tree is generous or a cat has feelings."

"Now just a minute," Julie said, taking the bait. "You know full well that your grandmother arrives for Christmas this evening, and she's bringing her cat with her and especially since Grandpa died she loves that silly cat more than life itself. So there will be no disparaging comments about cats in this house this Christmas. Do you understand?"

Jeremy smiled and nodded. But Rick was still fascinated with Mr. Ude. "So is Mr. Ude a cat lover?"

"Oh, I doubt that. He's allergic to nearly everything."

"So it wasn't talk about cats that made him lose his voice?"

"No. Religion"

"Religion? What does religion have to do with cats?"

"We weren't talking about cats. That was just an example. Somebody said that anthropomorphism is like giving human attributes to God when God isn't human. Then one of the kids who goes to that great big church chimed in and said that God is too human, because God is Jesus and Jesus is human. Then Rachel Jacobsen said that there is only one God and that God is so holy and mysterious that you can't even speak God's name out loud or make an image of God. And then somebody else said that that may be true but that the God of the Bible sure seems pretty human: mean and angry and kind of petty. And then one of the Muslim kids said that God is all merciful and somebody asked, 'But isn't Muhammad God?' and they said, 'No he's just a messenger, he's a prophet but he's not God,' and then somebody else said, 'I think that Jesus is like that, too,' and then people started to yell and Mr. Ude lost his voice. And then the bell rang."

"Saved by the bell, eh?" Rick chuckled. "Thank God."

Jeremy looked intrigued. "Yeah, you say that all the time... but do you really mean it? I'm not so sure any more."

"What I'm sure of," Julie interjected, "is that if we don't finish up and get in the car, we're going to be late getting Grandma. I hate to think of her wandering around the airport with that cat in tow."

"Speaking of which," Rick rejoined, "would it be too much trouble some year to ask the relatives to coordinate their arrivals a little bit? That 45-minute trip to the airport gets pretty old when we have to make it three days in a row."

"Just be glad they're coming at all. It will be wonderful to have everybody together."

"That's true. But I feel like a shuttle service."

Jeremy snorted. "That's kind of like the opposite of anthropomorphism: attributing to a person the characteristics of a non-person. You're a shuttle service."

"Actually," Rick replied, "it's just a simile, cousin to the metaphor. 'You're sitting there like a bump on a log. You are a pain in the butt.'" He smiled. "Let's get going."

Part II

At first, Gertrude the cat just stayed in her carrier. Grandmother Agnes had arrived none the worse for the wear; quite cheerful, in fact. Jeremy was more than delighted to see her. They had a very special connection. When he was just a toddler, Agnes had announced that "Grandma Agnes" was too big a mouthful for a small child; henceforth, he could call her "Gagnes." It stuck. As he got older from time to time he would call her "Your Gagnes." "Yes, Your Gagness...No, Your Gagness...Right away, Your Gagnes."

Agnes had taught English literature at a small liberal arts college. But she wasn't like most of Jeremy's teachers, who seemed to take themselves so seriously. Jeremy loved her. He never called her "Gagness" in public; it was a special thing between them.

In her own good time, Gertrude the cat emerged, stretched with an air of indifference and began to act as though she owned the place: rediscovering the litter box in the powder room, rubbing up against furniture, locating but disdaining the food and water dishes in the kitchen, and generally acclimating herself to her alternative environment. At least that's what it looked like she was doing. Jeremy was beginning to wonder about the true nature and origins of cat behavior.

When his parents went to the airport to collect Jeremy's older sister, Christina; her husband, Brett; and their newborn son, Joshua, Jeremy and Gagness had a chance to be alone. It wasn't long before the conversation turned to Mr. Ude.

"Listen, honey," Agnes said, "you just let that poor man alone. He's trying to teach English to a bunch of free-spirited ninth graders, and he's suffering enough—that's grounds for sainthood right there. He's not a referee in a class on comparative religions or dealing with a bunch of seminarians who are in love with their own brilliance and righteousness. Folks have fought about this God stuff way longer than either of us has been alive, and you can bet they'll go right on fighting about it."

"I know it's hard for Mr. Ude," Jeremy replied. "But what do you think about it?"

"About what, precisely?"

"About anthropomorphism. Do people just talk that way because it's the only way they have to talk about God? Or is God really like some people say—like an old man with a white beard sitting on a cloud and waiting for people to do stuff that's wrong so he can zap them? Or is God like Jesus? What do you really think?"

"Oh, honey," Agnes replied, "to tell you the truth, the older I get the less I care about all that stuff. People seem all ready to go to war, whether it's at school or with armies, over their beliefs. But their beliefs are a combination of images that amount to guesstimations. Anthropomorphism? Some people certainly overdo it. Trying to make God seem human they squeeze a great big mystery into a teeny little box and make God every bit as petty and mean as we are. Or we try so hard not to fall into that trap, we become so sophisticated that God is this vague, spiritual, undefined, cloud of beingness. Try to hug that!"

She reached out to pull her grandson to her. "Honey, when Grandpa died, I began to think about all that very differently. I cried and I cried and I cried. Some people blame God. But somewhere in there, when the tears were mostly gone, it seemed to me as though God was trying to sneak up on me to give me a hug. But I was so busy protecting myself that I couldn't feel it."

"What do you mean, Gagnes? That God has arms and legs and all that?"

"Oh no, honey. But I decided that anything worth calling 'God' has to be more than a mystery. If God is so much more than human, isn't God somehow at least as much as human? Anyway, I came to believe, feel—whatever—that God wants to get close to us on the inside. And when God does, it feels like a hug: like somebody who really, really knows you and really, really loves you."

"So did you feel a hug from God when Grandpa died? When did that happen?"

"Oh, it happened lots of times," she said, holding Jeremy tighter. "And it's happening right now."

Part III

One last trip to the airport. Jeremy's parents took Christina and her husband with them to collect Aunt Barb and Uncle Lou, the last of the arrivals. That left Agnes, Jeremy and, of course, Gertrude to look after little baby Joshua. Agnes had talked them into it. "You all just go on. Jeremy and I will look after this baby. It's good for you to get out of the house, and Jeremy and Joshua need a little uncle and nephew bonding time."

It was absolutely true that Jeremy was enthralled with Joshua. Some teenagers don't take much of a shine to infants: the crying and the smells and the constant attention they seem to need. But Jeremy was fascinated with Joshua. That first evening, he had changed his diaper…and Jeremy always seemed to show up around feeding time and was eager to take a hand at that.

Jeremy's sister, Christina, was amazed. "Well, little bro, you certainly seem to love this! You'll make a wonderful father someday." Jeremy just smiled.

And so he didn't protest when, after the others had left, Agnes rose from the couch and announced that she was going to bed. "I think the travel is catching up with me, and I'm not used to the kind of houseful we're going to have here for the next few days. You two will be just fine, I'm sure. But don't hesitate to holler if you need some help. Do you want me to take Gertrude up with me?" The cat lay curled at Jeremy's feet.

"No, she's fine right here. I thought cats were supposed to be jealous of babies."

"Now, Jeremy," Agnes replied. "That's shameless anthropomorphism." He laughed.

"Good night, honey," she said.

"Good night, Gagnes. Sweet dreams."

The next morning, Agnes emerged fresh as a daisy, eager for a full report from her grandson. "So," she said, "I take it you boys got along all right yesterday evening?"

"Oh, Gagnes! He's just amazing! When I hold his bottle he reaches out and grabs my hand…my finger, really—all of his perfect little fingers wrapped around one of mine. And those eyes! You could see forever in those eyes. And the strangest thing of all is that he trusts me. I want to warn him that I don't really know what I'm doing, that I'm really new at this, but he doesn't know and he doesn't care. He's just so… here."

Agnes sat quietly for minute. Then she smiled and sighed. "It's almost as though he's sneaking in there to give you a hug, isn't it? Right around your finger."

Jeremy laughed with delight. "It sure is, Gagnes! It sure is…What do you suppose Mr. Ude would say to that?"

"Well, that's the beauty of it, honey. He wouldn't have to say anything at all."

2013

This story, my last at Plymouth, deals with the painful realities and hopeful possibilities of change. I actually own the sport coat in question...and have not yet thrown it away...but maybe by the time you read this, I will have.

"All Things New"

Part I

"Well, that was certainly unpleasant," Don said.

Sarah knew a conversational ploy when she heard one. Her father had something on his mind and, sooner or later, she was going to hear the whole story. She took a deep breath and mentally settled in. "What was unpleasant, Dad?"

"This guy at the men's store...I don't think I've ever been

treated quite like that before."

"What did he do?"

"Well, I took in my blue herringbone sport coat—the one with the holes in the elbows?"

"Uh-huh. The one you've had since God was a small child?"

In the interests of telling his story, Don overlooked the slight, but he glared at his daughter over the top of his glasses to let her know she had transgressed. "It's a perfectly good coat except for the holes...and a couple of issues with the lining. I've always liked that coat. So I took it back to the place I bought it; well, not exactly the place I bought it, but the place that bought out the place I bought it. Anyway, they always used to pride themselves on making minor repairs or alterations to clothing they had sold—guaranteed for the life of the garment. So today I did what I had been thinking about doing for years, and I took my jacket in to see about having some patches put on the elbows."

He paused to give Sarah the opportunity to affirm the reasonableness of this. She was ominously silent. Don resumed his narrative.

"The clerk looked like he was about 17. He was sitting behind a desk. He didn't get up. I asked him about patches and he just said, 'You'd be better off with a new jacket.' I told him that I didn't want a new jacket, that I liked this one. He said, 'Even from across the room, anybody could tell that you hadn't bought that jacket in the last 10 years.' (I suppose that sounds like a long time to him.) He said, 'It's not exactly up-to-date.' I said, 'Take a good look at me. Do I look to you like somebody who cares about being up-to-date?' He didn't even look up. He just said, 'Certainly not.' I said, 'Well...if I am suddenly overcome with an irresistible urge to be fashionable, I'll know where to come.' And I left."

Sarah was silent. But Don was insistent: "Whatever happened to, 'The customer is always right'?"

Sarah responded quietly, almost tenderly: "The problem with 'the customer is always right,' Dad, is...sometimes they're not."

"What do you mean, 'Sometimes they're not'?"

"Just because the guy was rude doesn't mean he was wrong. That ratty old coat has had a good life, Dad. But patches? Even Jesus says not to put new patches on an old sport coat, right? Come on! They burn flags. Why don't you let that thing go out in a blaze of glory? I'll play 'Taps.'"

Don's eyes welled with tears that took them both by surprise. It was some time before he could speak. "It's not the coat," he said at last. "It's just that since your mother died, I guess I'm a lot more comfortable living in the past."

"It's been six years, Dad."

"I know it has. I know I need to move ahead with my life. But it's so hard to let go. I'm sorry. You don't need to hear all of this. You have your own life to worry about, you and Jake: a new marriage, a new house. I remember those days like they were yesterday. You don't need me dragging you down."

"Dad! It's OK. You're not dragging any of us down. You have to do what you have to do at your own speed. I've lost a mother, and I miss her every day, but I can't pretend to know what it's like to lose a spouse. But I do know what Mom would want for you. She'd want you to be happy. She does want you to be happy. Are you happy?"

He paused for a very long time. Sarah just waited.

At last he offered, "Some days are better than others. But sometimes I just get into this place where everything looks ugly and everybody is annoying. Christmas doesn't help very much. I know I can't bring back the past. But it's hard to trust the future when the present is just so damned lonely."

Part II

It didn't start well. Don hadn't even wanted to go to church, but Sarah and Jake were going and talked him into it. At least, he had thought, here I'll know what to expect. They do the same thing every year: same hymns, same lessons, same anthems, even. Church never changes.

But there was already somebody in their regular pew, and they had to sit clear on the other side of the sanctuary. At first, Don was comfortably entrenched on the end of a row. But a family with children came along, and a cheerful usher motioned to Don to scoot toward the center of the pew. Before he could protest, Jake and Sarah had already moved all the way into the middle and Don was guilted into moving, as well, his mood noticeably darkening. He always felt trapped in the center of a pew. Then he looked at his bulletin.

"All Things New," was the heading. "All Things New"? He gave it the quick once-over. The format was familiar: scripture readings interspersed with music—carols and anthems. But some of the lessons didn't look so familiar. There was the Creation story from Genesis...then an ominous portion from Isaiah, "Do not remember the former things, or consider the things of old. I am about to do a new thing; now it springs forth, do you not perceive it?" Huh. With a deepening sense of foreboding, he let his eyes dance on down the page. Luke 2: right...the shepherds. Matthew 2: OK, that's the wise men. Wait a minute...what's this? Revelation 21? Oh, please!

He looked it over: "'See, the home of God is among mortals. [God] will dwell with them... [God] will wipe away every tear from their eyes. Death will be no more; mourning and crying and pain will be no more, for the first things have passed away.' And the one who was seated on the throne said, 'See, I am making all things new.'" Don rolled his eyes. Who in the world felt the need to mess with Christmas Eve?

As if in answer to this silent plea for accountability, suddenly the pastor was standing out in front of the congregation with a hand-held microphone. "Good evening, everybody," she said. "Merry Christmas!"

"Merry Christmas," a few brave souls responded tentatively.

"As some of you may have noticed, we're already past time for the prelude to have started. I have just heard from the organist. Her car died on the freeway." An audible groan went up from the congregation. "Her husband has gone to get her, she'll drive here in his car and he'll wait for the tow truck. She isn't far away. We should be underway in about 10 minutes. Sorry for the delay. We could start without the preacher, but not without the organist! Feel free to visit among yourselves for a few minutes."

This, to be sure, was new! Don shook his head, sighed and chuckled to himself as a voice to his left said, "Excuse me. Do you happen to have a napkin or a Kleenex or something? I'm just getting used to the full time grandmother gig and I have obviously ventured out unprepared."

Don fumbled in his pockets and produced a travel-size packet of tissues. As he turned to hand it to her their eyes met briefly: a spark there. He glanced away quickly. Then he said, "Keep the change." She laughed. Nice laugh.

She turned away to tend to a moist emergency with one of the small children...but a few moments later she was back. "Is there anything on earth more wound up than a kid on Christmas Eve?" she asked cheerfully.

"It's been quite a while for me," Don replied, pointing to Sarah as he added, "but I sure remember when my daughter here was little. Special memories."

"Do you belong to this church?" she responded. "We've just moved here and we're interested in finding a place where we can get involved. Do you know anything about this church?"

"Oh yes," Don replied. "I hardly know where to begin. I've belonged here for 25 years, and I have a lot of precious memories in this room. My wife and I joined just before we had Sarah baptized. She was confirmed here. She was married here last fall. And Barbara, my wife...well, we had her funeral here, too, and a lot of Christmases. Barbara and I were very involved—committees and so forth. But I need to do something different."

As Don listened to himself talk, he wondered, "Why am I telling her all of this," but he kept right on. "There always seems to be a lot going on here. We just started a program to house homeless families here in the building from time to time. I thought I might help with that."

She looked at him knowingly. "It wouldn't happen to be called 'Family Promise,' would it?"

"Yes, actually I think that is the name. How did you know?"

"We were considering it at my church in Boulder just before I left. It's a lot of work, but it looks absolutely amazing—the way different churches in a community work together to house and feed homeless families and surround them with services and support. We were right on the verge of joining as a congregation when I decided to move here to be closer to the grandchildren. It was a tough choice to kind of start over. But I'm really glad I'm here."

"You mentioned Boulder. Were you there a long time? What's your story?"

Don had hardly noticed that the lights had dimmed and the prelude had begun.

Part III

How could he not have known? What else could have been in a box that size? For the briefest moment, Don flirted with being annoyed. Then he looked at his daughter and laughed with joy and love.

It was a nice sport coat: not a herringbone, but a tasteful tweed, built to wear like iron…with patches already on the sleeves. "Good God!" He exclaimed. "How professorial! I'm going to have start smoking a pipe!" Then he really laughed. "You can bury me in this thing!" he blurted out.

"Could be," Sarah replied. "But you've got a lot of living to do in it first. You need to get to work on finding places to wear it."

Don nodded.

But the best part was the backstory that had tumbled out. Sarah had gone to the same store, the scene of the crime. And as fate would have it had found the same clerk, who remembered Don a good deal better than Don had remembered him; in fact, his guess on Don's size had been right on the money. And the clerk had been so surprised! Sarah quoted him exactly, "Pardon me for being so direct, but I am astonished that you think your father would want to patronize this store. Our conversation was…"

Sarah completed the thought: "Unpleasant?"

"Yes! You could certainly say it was unpleasant. Your father seemed to be having a pretty bad day." They all had a pretty good laugh over that one.

But Don liked his new coat…not as well as the old one,

mind you, but well enough for now. It would take some getting used to and need some breaking in. But there was time enough for that…plenty of time.

Made in the USA
Charleston, SC
03 November 2014